G000143639

CUSTOMER EXPERIENCE:

IT'S NOT THAT EASY

**Customer Experience
Programs for B2B Companies**

HARRY F BUNN

It's Not That Easy
Customer Experience Programs
for B2B Companies

Bunn, Harry F.

Key words: Customer experience, Customer satisfaction, Voice of
the Customer, market research, strategy, corporate culture, CEO

Published by:
RONIN Development Corporation
101 College Road East
Princeton NJ 08540 USA

609-452-0060

Copyright 2014
All rights reserved. This document, or parts thereof, may not be
reproduced in any form without the written permission of the publisher

ISBN: 0-615-99370-2
ISBN-13: 978-0-615-99370-6
Library of Congress Control Number: 2014908655
RONIN Corporation, Princeton, NJ
Printed in the United States of America

This book is dedicated to past and present members of RONIN and the clients we serve.

I would like to extend my deep appreciation to Dr. Bob Harlow who contributed the section on analytics and Ms. Jenny Cai who reviewed the text and added the aspects on social media.

Also, Jennie Koval who worked through the text, battling Microsoft Word as she did so.

TABLE OF CONTENTS

PREFACE

Over the past 27 years, RONIN Corporation has undertaken consulting and research engagements for clients in the Business-to-Business (B2B) space relating to their markets and their customer relationships. We have worked with some of the largest and most sophisticated corporations in the United States and throughout the world, including all the major information technology companies.

In that time we have learnt a lot. We have approached Customer Experience in some innovative ways, and we have also dealt with the practicality of how to get it done in large corporations where the organizational structure and philosophy do not always match what is needed to achieve success.

The approach and philosophy for Customer Experience that are set out in this book form a logical path to achieving the optimal Customer Experience, using this as a lynchpin of the vendor's strategy. We have worked on all aspects of this approach but not as one clear, singular strategy for one vendor.

In fact, no vendor currently has it all together. To do so is not easy, but the benefits are incredible.

If this book inspires one vendor to put in the hard work to get it right, it will have been worth it.

Customer Experience programs, if implemented well, are significant competitive differentiators. As such, many of the details regarding how they have been implemented are confidential, as are the names of many of the companies whose practices are discussed in this book.

PART 1:

B2B Customer Experience

1: WHAT IS CUSTOMER EXPERIENCE?

In January 2007, Nokia was the worldwide leader in cell phones, and Motorola was a fairly close second. Then Steve Jobs stood up and announced that Apple had the iPhone. The tech giants laughed (for a short time). "Apple is going to compete in the cutthroat cell-phone marketplace where margins are low?" Likewise, the cell-phone manufacturers also laughed. "What does Apple know about telephony, low-cost manufacturing, and mass marketing to consumers?"

Steve Jobs, however, made a clear statement that it was all about the user experience.

The world loves to buzz with the latest technology, the latest CEO error, the latest political gaff, and the latest management approach to gaining success in savage, unpredictable global markets. In the past year or two, the new phrase has been "Customer Experience."

In the corporate world the new game in town is engaging the customer. It is clear that the minimal growth in GDP globally reflects stable or reduced spending in most industries, which results in low or no growth in the top-line revenue numbers of the major corporations.

But these corporations need to show results to bolster their stock prices, so they have turned to cost reduction. This can come from buying less expensive components—through excellent supply-chain management and, frankly, draconian purchasing habits. In addition, there has been a general reduction in workforce costs by replacing people with technology and/or using the global workforce marketplace to find lower-cost workers than the United States or European countries can provide.

Over time there will be a leveling of wage rates. Rates in China are already higher, influencing clothing manufacturers who are driven by the high costs in urban cities in the east of China to shift offshore to Bangladesh and Myanmar. In India, back-office processing and call centers too have been hit by rapidly increasing wage rates and significant staff turnover as the limited numbers of educated and experienced staff change jobs to gain increased salaries.

Corporations are being pushed back toward increasing the top line since increasing the cost savings is running out of steam.

However, customers have been able to gain power from the global, Internet-based economy. They can search for specific products and, with a few clicks, find the lowest cost. Using the same websites, they can become aware of brands they may not have heard of previously.

Companies have become aware of the need to forge strong ties with their customers, to provide them an incrementally better experience than their competitors, and to foster loyalty based on customer leadership. That way they can displace competitors or at least gain a greater share of the spend than their competitors.

Customer Experience

Recently, the concept of Customer Experience has become a major part of company strategy and implementation. The definition in Wikipedia is useful:

The total sum of conscious and unconscious events which the customer perceives of the vendor. Every interaction creates additions to the cumulative experience.

Forrester Research defines Customer Experience as having three elements:

- Fulfills the need – a basic threshold but not a winning factor
- Easy – to buy, to implement, to use, to get help and support
- Enjoyable – an emotion often embodied in the phase "to delight" (rather than just satisfy) the customer

A vendor hopes that each of their customers will:

- Recommend the vendor/product to others
- Purchase from that vendor again
- Continue to use that vendor
- Increase the percentage of their overall spend with that vendor

That sounds like customer satisfaction! And in most companies that is exactly what it is.

However, whereas a customer satisfaction program can be managed by a group within a company's organization with little need for input from others nor top-level support, Customer Experience is fundamentally different.

It reflects and requires a <u>culture</u> that is embraced by the CEO and accepted by all employees and agents of the company. It is not just a "program." It is a <u>philosophy</u>.

Customer satisfaction measures just one aspect of the experience—satisfaction. Customer Experience is an <u>emotion</u> (normally based on fact), it is <u>holistic</u>, it is <u>relative</u>, and it is based on <u>expectations</u>. Thus, the questions being asked to measure it need to be more open-ended and not just: "On a 7-point scale, rate the quality of the product."

In addition, customer satisfaction programs typically test the satisfaction level of the account team's main contact. Customer Experience is the total experience of <u>all people</u> within the customer organization, and the Customer Experience Program (CEP) is the mechanism for establishing objectives, measuring their achievement, and driving actions to (cost effectively) improve it.

In most companies, the Customer Experience Program is an outgrowth of the customer satisfaction program. This is a totally valid approach. Customer Experience is a logical extension—there is a team in place, and the methods for measurement, data collection, reporting, and action are established and proven.

However, a real Customer Experience Program goes a lot further. It is a way of embodying the customer in the culture, strategy, and tactics of the company. The measurement aspects are important as are the actions and feedback directed to the customers, but omitting the overarching aspects across the company will not optimize the full value that a company can receive from this approach. Customer Experience should be implemented across the organization, and there is a lot of up-front work required to establish the framework that will act as a foundation for the program.

One, but only one, aspect of the CEP is measurement of the Customer Experience. Often executive management wants to resolve this down to a single numeric score—the CE index. This can comprise an aggregated answer to a single question (e.g., the Net Promoter Score (NPS) or a composite of several factors). The NPS question asks simply whether the customer would recommend the vendor.

Definitions

To avoid confusion, we have used the term "customer" to depict the company that comprises the buyer and user of the products/services, and we have used the term "vendor" to depict the seller/provider of these products and services. To shorten the text, we have abbreviated the term Customer Experience to "CE" and the Customer Experience Program to "CEP." Because a vendor can sell products and/or services in the B2B framework, we have used the term "products" to encompass both.

B2C implies a business-to-consumer relationship, whereas the focus of this book in on B2B, business-to-business.

2: WHY IS BUSINESS TO BUSINESS CE DIFFERENT?

The bottom line for Customer Experience is that most CEPs and approaches are based on a consumer or B2C model. Many people, including some consultants, really do not understand the fundamental difference between B2C and B2B. Several programs that have failed have done so, in large part, because of this.

In the B2C world, CE is often associated with "ease of use." Steve Jobs described the iPhone in terms of the user experience, but aspects of the Apple success story extend this to a range of aspects of the product itself—the ease of use, the flexibility of new touch-screen technology, the quality and resolution of the display, the Apple store experience, and even the "cool" packaging in which the iPhone arrives. All of these product elements made the experience exciting and fulfilled the promises of a great experience. But the B2B world is different.

In the consumer world:

- The transaction value is low (in the case of McDonald's, it is a couple dollars).
- The customer base is huge (often in the millions).
- The customers are about equal in their buying power (they all spend about the same).

- The transactions are quick and spontaneous, often based on emotion rather than reason.
  - Customers have little power other than to buy or not to buy—they can rarely bargain individually, nor can they expect special discounts or faster delivery.
  - Customers treat each purchase separately and base their overall view of the seller on each individual experience—one might use a restaurant for many years and then, after one bad experience, never go back.

The Customer Experience then is geared toward individual transactions, and vendors can (and should) use "big data" based on, in some cases, millions of transactions to predict how the selling process and the use can be incrementally improved.

The B2B world is very different:

Larger transaction value
The average transaction value is high. Other than buying a home, the highest purchase for a consumer is an automobile. In the B2B world, products and services can be purchased for hundreds of thousands or even millions of dollars.

Smaller number of customers
Even when a company is selling to small businesses, their customer base is typically in the thousands rather than the millions.

80/20 rule-based
Not all B2B customers are equal. McDonald's spend per customer is fairly flat. In B2B, some companies and governments can spend orders of magnitude more than other, smaller companies.

The 80/20 rule applies to B2B. Developed originally by the Italian economist Pareto, this rule observes that 80% of the spend will be from just

20% of customers, with the other 20% spread over the other 80% of customers.

This allows, and requires, that companies focus on the 20%—their largest customers. Companies need to segment their customer base so that Customer Experience is resourced more to the more important customers and less to the less important ones.

In the Customer Experience Program, it is fundamental that you separate the two (or more) groups of customers and treat them separately—and measure them separately.

Often a direct sales force with vested interests
Certainly when you buy a car, there is an assertive salesperson. But because they only sell a car to an individual every few or more years, they do not focus on building and growing a relationship.

In B2B, building the relationship is most important and is the basis for the Customer Experience.

This is often done with account teams or salespeople who nurture the relationship and, in many cases, spend time learning the customer's business, challenges, and problems.

The B2B sales teams, however, usually have a vested interest in keeping management and others away from their customer contacts. In addition, as with the car salespeople, they are very keen to receive high customer-satisfaction scores, and when there is a problem with the account, they will attempt to find reasons to prevent the satisfaction interview from taking place.

Longer lead time
In a B2C environment, the lead time is usually short. Someone may search the Internet for a product, compare a few, get the best price, and buy it. It

may be delivered the next day and be in use immediately. In a retail experience, the lead time may be even shorter.

For B2B, an RFP is often drawn up, approved, and sent out to qualified vendors who submit proposals. These are considered, recommendations are made, management submits approvals, and finally a purchase is made—perhaps with a significant time before delivery and implementation. This can take months or even years.

"Professional" buying
In a B2C environment, the buyer is an individual who will assess the product and price and then purchase. In B2B, there are a number of people involved, and in the past few years, more and more have come to use a professional purchasing group. Purchasing has only one task—negotiate the lowest price. Often their bonuses are set on the basis of savings they have been able to extract from their suppliers.

We have not found a case where these people are included in customer satisfaction programs whereas they often make the final decision. Even though this is likely to be based greatly on price, their input in the satisfaction measurement is important.

Complexity of the products
Along with the high unit prices and the long lead time to decision, many B2B sales are of complex products that can take a long time to implement. Sometimes the implementation process is expected to be difficult and requires the customer to have certain skills or to use outside contractors to assist.

In addition, the people who will use the product have often not been involved in the decision making, which is rare in the B2C world.

Fundamentally different decision-making process and organization
When consumers buy, they may consult friends or other family members, but usually there is just one decision maker. In a B2B situation, there are

usually multiple people involved—a technical recommender, the end user, purchasing, finance, legal, and executives. The purchase may be ad hoc, but more than likely it will use funding from a budget.

Is it any surprise that a CEO with a consumer background can flounder in B2B and vice versa? Is it also any surprise that the packaged approaches to CE based on a B2C model do not play well in the B2B space?

Companies with hybrid B2B and B2C models
Many companies are hybrids—some products are sold to consumers and others to businesses (e.g., electric generators).

One of the things that causes a CEP to fail is when a company uses one approach for both consumers and B2B. The approach to each has to be different. This is a clear case when "one size does NOT fit all."

What is a CE program in B2B and why is it so complex?

A B2C Customer Experience is fairly simple.

Picture a lemonade stand. The business model is simple: the little girl provides lemonade from a lemonade stand for cash.

The Customer Experience is singular and short. The experience relates to the little girl selling the lemonade and might be expressed as:

- Friendly
- Clean
- Good quality product
- Acceptable price
- Good location
- Nice glasses to drink from
- Cute little girl

The experience also stretches out a little to include "word of mouth," signs, and local advertisements on notice boards. It also includes comparisons with other lemonade stands and memories of the little girls in other activities.

But many consumer products have a more complex Customer Experience. Let's consider the iPhone.

What are the experiences that a potential buyer has? These relate to **touch points.** He/she might:

- Read a *Wall Street Journal* article about the new iPhone
- Go to Apple's website
- Watch an interview with Tim Cook
- Use the iTunes website
- Listen while a friend "talks up" the new iPhone
- Visit an Apple retail store
- Check out a competitive smart phone in a carrier store
- See a TV show about manufacturing facilities in China
- See a news program about the new iPhone
- Buy the iPhone

- Sign up for a network plan
- Activate the phone
- Use the iPhone

What impact will a negative experience at the Apple store have? Will difficulties in transferring iTunes files to a new PC affect the new iPhone purchase? If the network plan sign-up is difficult, does this impact the customer's view of Apple?

In both these cases, there is a single **product** and a single buyer (although peers may have an influence). The complexity comes from the product's "**touch points.**"

In the B2B world, there are often multiple products and multiple touch points adding complexity. There is also another dimension of complexity in the **roles** within the customer organization that contribute to the total experience. There are many people or roles involved in the experience at the customer end—not just the "decision maker."

As well as the many products, touch points, and roles that affect the perception of the experience, there are two other aspects—the **customer journey** and the position of the products in their **life cycle**. A customer may be approaching the product purchase for the first time and will need to understand the product category and what the options are. Other customers may be well down the "journey" path and be concentrating on aspects of usage. While each customer may be at different points, the product overall will be at a point in its life cycle—embryonic, growth, mature, or decline—and the importance of the various touch points will be different based on this factor. In the embryonic stage, concentration is needed in the early customer journey steps. As the product matures, these become less important unless the vendor is targeting new users in, say, a mature market.

The B2B complexity with four dimensions

Many people/roles in the customer organization

Buyers/decision makers
Procurement
Users
Managers
Finance
Legal
C-suite executives

Many touch points

Sales people
Channels
Web site
Advertisements
PR
Peer opinions
Blogs
Consultants
Social networking

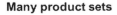

Many product sets

Customer Journey and Life cycle

I said it wasn't easy!

When we address CE, we have to review all the dimensions, and we can do that from any angle.

For one company, we developed an approach revolving around the customer journey product and the product life cycle. We first positioned each of the vendor's products against the elements of the relevant customer journey and then applied importance based on the position in the life cycle. The chart below, for product x, sets this out with the weight of the line showing those journey elements that are most important. Product x is mature, so the most important aspects were delivery and implementation and use, with less important factors in the earlier parts of the life cycle.

Different product/service sets will require different emphasis in the customer journey based on stage of maturity

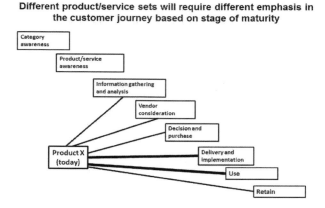

We then considered the role dimension. In the second chart we depicted where a chief marketing officer interfaces—in the very early days of an embryonic product and then in the use of the product. They do not gather information on the product that might be used (a CRM system), nor do they have any influence on the vendor consideration.

Each "player" in the customer organization has a different focus

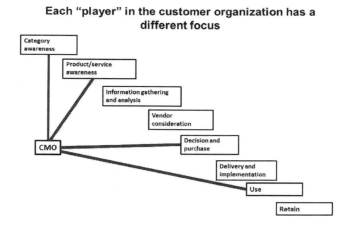

The third chart shows an analysis by a specific touch point—in this case, the website. This is used mostly during the early stages of the customer journey and the early stages in the product life cycle.

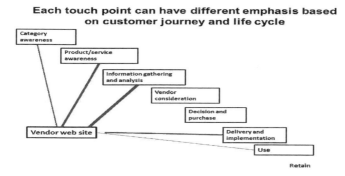

Each touch point can have different emphasis based on customer journey and life cycle

These dimensions become the framework for our CE Program.

Social media and big data in Customer Experience

Many articles on Customer Experience today point out the importance of social media in understanding the Customer Experience. They then go on to point out how blogs, tweets, etc. can be analyzed using text analytics software and other "big data" approaches.

This is just fine in the B2C world, but it is less useful in the B2B world. We address this further in Chapter 14.

3: THE ELEMENTS OF A CEP

There are three major parts to the introduction of a successful CEP:

- Customer focus – embedding the customer in the vendor's culture and strategies
- The framework within which the program will be rolled out
- Implementation – measurement, the actions to take optimal corrective action, and feedback to the customers

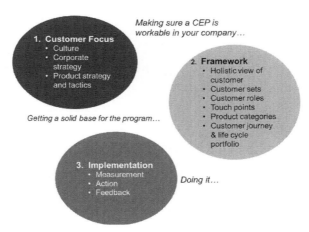

The focus on Customer Experience needs to be part of the company **culture**—it is not just paying lip service to this. Everyone in the vendor's organization should be thinking and asking the question, "What will we do to make the Customer Experience better?"

Customer Experience needs to be built into the **strategy** of the company and then into **product or business unit strategies and tactics**.

There needs to be a **framework** to which the strategies and measurement aspects are anchored.

- A **holistic view of the customer** (and prospects) – who are they, and what are their behaviors, attitudes, needs, and wants?
- **Customer sets** – what are the logical groupings for our customers? Based on size? Revenue to us? Margin?
- What **roles** are important in the customer organizations – this is of little importance in B2C, but for B2B it is fundamental and is often missed by traditional customer satisfaction programs. It goes beyond just the buyer and includes users, procurement, legal, and senior executives.
- **Touch points** – what are the specific touch points we use to provide the Customer Experience (e.g., direct sales people, website, call center)?
- **Customer journey** – the progression in the Customer Experience for an individual customer
- **Life cycle portfolio** – the experience requirements will be different at different phases in the product life cycle.

The **implementation** starts with **measuring** activities in terms of the customer's view of the experience. The traditional methods of market research work well here, but there are other methods that can be added.

Following identification of problems (either one-off or systemic), there needs to be an optimization of the **actions** to be taken to resolve them. The actions need to be tracked to ensure that they are effective, and future measurement with customers is necessary to verify the fixes.

Finally **feedback** is required to the customers. They need to be told that their comments have been heard and acted on. If the problem cannot be resolved for whatever reason, feedback regarding what was considered and then rejected can still be communicated and is far better than just ignoring the complaint.

A vendor's embrace of CE is across a continuum. It can be anywhere from a simple customer satisfaction study run once a year to a total CEP (where the customer satisfaction methodology is used for one part of the program—to gain feedback from customers). What is missing from this is the experience with the product over time, the experience in the customer journey to using the product—awareness, consideration, alternatives, plus the various touch points (e.g., customer service a few weeks in when the product has a problem or something cannot be made to work). Customer satisfaction relies on a simple survey methodology and can be invasive.

CE covers the whole life cycle, the whole set of touch points, the whole product and service set from the vendor (including its interaction) and all the players who are involved. It should go beyond the traditional survey and accept inputs from a wide variety of sources (e.g., customer service, the sales force, automated responses, social media, and web scanning).

No wonder it isn't easy.

Currently CE is fragmented

Few, if any, vendors operate without some form of customer focus. Advancing that to a full CEP has taken a number of different paths, and sometimes, the resulting program is not optimal since some of the logical steps have been missed or have been implemented without the CEP concept in mind.

There is an old Irish joke with the punch line, "You know, sir, if I was going to Balbriggan, I wouldn't start from here at all."

Source: http://www.abitoblarney.com/irishjokes.htm

In the same way, to get to a full CEP, the path will usually be determined from the starting point.

Most B2B CEPs that we have observed are outgrowths from a customer satisfaction program. This is both positive and negative.

On the positive front, there is an organization already in place that can implement the next spin, and a lot of the mechanics for determining the customer viewpoint are already in place. If the customer satisfaction program is well accepted and used to make changes in the organization—with the customer satisfaction management having a "seat at the table" in executive discussions—the transition is easier. If the customer satisfaction approach is not held in great regard and is viewed as a low-cost way of creating a "feel good" scorecard and little else, it may be better to start from another angle and, at a suitable time, transition the existing approach.

One company that develops software for electronic circuit design has taken a different approach. The CEO infused in all employees a set of customer-centric systems, processes, and culture. He adopted a five-part strategy focusing on areas he believed were the main challenges for his company. These were not discovered from market research but by internal workshops with the account teams. In fact, their customers were chip makers and very limited in numbers.

The areas for the CEP were related to touch points:

- Customer education
- Online customer portal
- Support centers
- Field application engineers
- Professional services organization

An initial "diagnostic study" was used to determine the metrics against which each of these could be measured.

The program was managed through a central CRM system and was recognized as a partial solution. The existing customer satisfaction program was adapted to provide ongoing measurement of the program.

PART 2:

Customer Focus

It would take a very foolhardy CEO to assert that the customer is not important. Going back a century or so, salespeople were exhorted with the phrase, "The customer is king," and this philosophy has continued. Indeed, one CEO of a lower-end retail jewelry chain in the UK joked at a company dinner that his company's products were "crap" and their customers were stupid for buying them. The media picked up the story, and the CEO was fired within two weeks.

Most CEOs will say they are customer focused, but this is not a black or white situation. Some vendors fully embrace the customer while others do so to a lesser extent. Where they lie on the spectrum of customer focus is the important aspect and leads to the level of Customer Experience Program that is most appropriate for the vendor.

Interestingly, Apple has positioned itself as a product-driven company. They will engineer and deliver the best technology with a great user experience. Of course, the customer is fundamental, but they believe that they can provide products the customers will love. This "build the field and they will come" philosophy has obviously been highly successful.

The CEP has to be in line with the philosophy and culture of the vendor. If a new CEO wishes to change the culture of the company he/she is coming into, the CEP can play an important role in making the change, or it can operate against a philosophy already in place.

The absolute first step in developing or modifying a CEP is to understand where the company is (or wishes to be) on the customer focus spectrum. In the B2C marketplace, there are few, if any, situations where a small number of customers dominate sales. Customer focus can be a more mechanical approach. In B2B, getting the customer focus right is fundamental.

The CEO tends to be focused on internals—people, organization structure, etc.—and he/she must focus down onto two or three major simple issues: quality and throughput, low-cost producer, best marketer of financial services for selected target customers, or superior branch network, for example. Or "the Customer Experience."

The following transcript is from a *60 Minutes* episode on Amazon that aired on Dec. 1, 2013. Charlie Rose is the correspondent who interviewed Jeff Bezos, CEO of Amazon.

Charlie Rose: Tell me what is Amazon today?

Jeff Bezos: I would define Amazon by our big ideas, which are customer centricity, putting the customer at the center of everything we do, and invention. We like to pioneer, we like to explore, we like to go down dark alleys and see what's on the other side.

The customer focus index

So where is your company on the customer focus continuum?

We have asked vendors to position themselves on this simple 1-7 scale.

Score	Our beliefs relating to the customer	Our attitude towards customers	Appropriate program
1	We dominate our marketplace and our customers have to buy from us. We place little focus on our customers	They are a pain in the a***	Low level customer satisfaction program conducted once every few years
2	Our customers are important to us but we do not use their input to determine our actions and strategy	They pay the bills so we have to put up with them	
3	Our customers are important to us and we measure customer satisfaction. We do not rely on input from them to drive our company strategy	We need to keep our costs down in dealing with customers	
4	We track customers and take what they tell us seriously. We use a scorecard to determine how well we are doing	We try to keep them happy and use basic satisfaction programs	Continuous customer satisfaction program
5	We have a strong relational dialog with our customers but position ourselves as leading them rather than them dictating what we do	We have programs in place to track their satisfaction and loyalty levels and we act on their issues	
6	Customer experience in in our top three areas of focus	We maintain an active dialog with our customers to understand them and their needs	
7	We are totally responsive to our customers in terms of products, service, marketing,. We rely on their continuous input to evolve our business	Pleasing them is the most important goal we have as a company	Full CEP

Obviously different people in the vendor organization will have different views, and the collecting of these different views makes for an invaluable exercise. We recommend that the data be collected in a structured, quantitative manner so that analysis can be undertaken across geographies, functional units, management hierarchy, etc. The differences will allow action to be taken to reinforce the CEO's fundamental view. If he/she believes that the vendor is a type 6 company, and the sales force believes that the company operates as a type 3 company, there is a lot of realignment to be done.

The survey needs to cover all groups and functions within the company.

Let's now address the three areas of customer focus:

- Culture
- Corporate strategy
- Product strategy and tactics

4: CULTURE

A customer-centric culture is an engrained belief across the vendor that the customer is fundamental to the success of the company. In some vendors, lip service is paid to this, and the culture reverts to doing the least possible to "keep the customers happy" rather than embracing the relationship with the customers to provide value for both sides.

Culture is an emotional aspect, and it can be very difficult to change this. Sometimes, however, something simple can bring about the change.

> Most American airlines have been through significant turbulence in their fortunes, and in many cases this has affected the attitude of their people. The result has been that those interacting with their business (and consumer) customers do not provide the expected service levels and, even more important, the expected attitude. The flight attendants have seen pay cuts and have responded by regarding their jobs as mundane and disrespected by management.

> Many years back, flying was fun. The flight attendants were happy and wanted to do everything they could to make the passengers' flight enjoyable. This is a "culture thing." The flight attendants are no longer hired and trained to bring that attitude to their work. Exceptions can be found in the newer airlines like JetBlue and Southwestern, which from the beginning have embraced the "enjoyable service" culture.

In terms of changing culture, some years ago, British Airways moved through a period when a customer-centric attitude was not part of their culture, and they lost market share to Virgin Atlantic and other airlines. They changed. A strong message came down from the executive office that this was expected and that the customer was fundamental to the airline's success. The change happened almost overnight. Part of the rapid acceptance was that employees like to have their customers happy rather than miserable. It is up to management to embrace the customer focus and then support it with actions. The "nickel and diming" that has gone on in a lot of the airlines supports the belief that the customer is unimportant to the airline.

While there are a few situations where the company culture is not driven by the beliefs of the CEO, this is rare. Typically, it is the CEO who establishes the culture. But that person must ensure that the concept is not just held in the corporate offices or the boardroom but spread throughout the company and supported by appropriate actions. The phrase all of us hear a lot when contacting customer service is, "Your call is important to us," followed by a complex IVR system and eventually an agent who has been recruited based on low cost rather than expertise, experience, and attitude. This is a classic example of how the actions do not match the message.

It is difficult for an entrenched CEO to bring about a change in culture, even if it revolves around customer centricity. It is much easier when a new CEO comes into a company. If he/she finds a well-entrenched culture, the options are to embrace the existing, make minor changes that can be become more major changes over time, or make a radical change. If the company is in trouble before the new CEO joins, he/she will have a greater and more defensible ability to make the changes.

Culture relates to values, beliefs, and attitudes, so influencing and changing this can be difficult. There are also questions regarding how ethical it is to try to change it. However, behavior is something different. This can legitimately be changed by training and by incentive. Telling staff that they should embrace the customer and do everything to make their experience better may not fly with some people, but providing incentives such as an award for the most customer focused person of the week, etc. can support the behavior that a customer focused company requires.

To introduce a customer focus culture, the CEO needs to prepare the principles of behavior into a written document that is distributed across the organization. This needs to be followed by education in small groups, workshops, etc. A CE spokesperson may even join all the strategy sessions and continue to ask the question, "How does that improve the Customer Experience?" This is a little like the slave in ancient Roman triumph parades who would continually say, "Memento mori"—you are only mortal—to the honored general to ensure that the triumph did not go to his head.

Reward systems are fundamental, but there is a risk that managers will attempt to "game the system" rather than embrace the culture that is being implemented. When managers' bonuses are impacted by Customer Experience or customer satisfaction scores, there can be some harmful byproducts.

An interview* with Randall L. Stephenson, chairman and CEO at AT&T, recently explored how a new culture was introduced into AT&T. Randall's comment related to a culture of innovation, but the approaches and processes he describes work well with customer centricity as well.

> I tell people that it cannot be a culture of don'ts. A culture of integrity and trust is a culture of dos. Do the right thing and don't get focused and enamored with the don'ts.

> In fact, when I bring somebody in to the senior leadership team, they're required to come into my office whether they're hired off the street or whether they're promoted to the position. I spend 15 minutes with

them and it is 15 minutes and 15 minutes only. We do not talk about what my expectations are for them in the role they're about to enter. We talk about one thing, and that is their responsibility as an officer of this company. I communicate with them something very directly and that is: Becoming an officer in this company does not give you new privileges, it gives you a higher level of responsibility and it actually requires you to step up your integrity.

You have to drive the culture and bring people into the business that you trust not only to work with integrity in the professional environment, but live that way and exemplify those outside of work. Once you have what you believe to be a sound culture of trust and integrity at the highest levels, you can begin to drive that down into the organization.

* Reported in BGS International Exchange Fall 2013.

5: CORPORATE STRATEGY

Each vendor has its own approach to developing and implementing corporate strategy. If CE becomes a driving aspect of this strategy, it lays the foundation for a successful CEP.

It is easy for the CEO and executive committee to indicate the importance of the customer, but how does this become embedded in the corporate strategy? We shall address product line/business unit strategy and tactics in the next chapter.

Vision and mission come first—big, bold statements about the values the vendor holds and what it sees for its future. These statements need to reflect the customer focus.

So what are the elements of corporate strategy?

The following is a supporting structure that we have used for developing and documenting corporate strategy:

The business model is an integration of these four elements:

Products: What products/services do we develop and sell now and in the future? Within which categories do we participate?

Markets: To whom do we sell our products/services? Large companies? Small companies? Specific industries? Which geographies? Countries? Regions? To which roles/departments do we sell? Head of IT? CFO? CMO? Manufacturing management? Who influences the sale? Who signs off on the sale? Who can veto the sale? Who uses the product? Are our prospects different from our customers?

Offers: This comprises all aspects of sales and marketing. How are the products differentiated? How are they positioned? How are they packaged? What are the customer touch points? How do we market? What is our direct sales vs. channel strategy? How do we price?

Internals: What resources do we have? What limitations do we have? Human resources (e.g., how good are our sales people)? Capital? Manufacturing capability? Economies of scale and scope? Development? Joint ventures? Strategic alliances? Speed—growth, development? What are our core differentiators?

Documentation of these elements will often require a matrix addressing each of the product sets. Do we offer the whole product range to all customers in the same "offer" scenario? Not doing so may be a challenge and an opportunity. Can we leverage aspects of our "internals" to optimize revenues and profitability? Do we need to address certain product sets fundamentally differently? If so, should we consider divesting these?

A fifth aspect of our strategic review is to consider the same four elements for major and emerging competitors.

The corporate strategy then becomes some overarching directions, identification of the first steps toward change and the portfolio of businesses that will achieve the overall goals. Most companies, particularly the larger ones, have a portfolio of businesses at different stages in the life cycle: some are mature businesses contributing solid profitability but not growing a lot of revenue; others are in the embryonic phase and require investment, involve risk, and lack probability though they are growing fast.

In one case, a Fortune 500 company that we were working with was proud of their new fast-growing businesses until we modeled them and saw that, despite a high growth rate, the base was small and the revenue that might be expected over the coming five years would not make up for the decline in their traditional businesses.

The bottom line for the CEP is that documenting the corporate strategy will allow for an understanding of how customer focused the vendor is and will also provide the groundwork for the CEP framework—product categories, customer sets, and touch points.

In a customer-centric company, strategy is developed with the customer at the forefront. During strategy development sessions the question that should be asked continually is, "How does this affect the customer?" This should not be an afterthought. The Customer Experience becomes an embodiment of the strategy, and the strategy is built around it. The strategy is built from the foundation of the company's culture. Without a customer-centric culture, the Customer Experience is relegated to an afterthought.

6: PRODUCT STRATEGY AND TACTICS

Corporate strategy tends to involve "big thoughts." At a product group level, the strategy becomes more real and tangible.

Here Customer Experience can play an even more important role. During the planning sessions, the product life cycle can be addressed and superior Customer Experience planned out, matching touch points to customer sets and to customer roles.

In one planning session, the conversation went like this:

> We are in the early stages of the life cycle. Customers are generally aware of the category but have little awareness of what products are emerging and who the vendors are likely to be. At this stage the most useful roles in the customer organization are the technical people and the functional heads. We shall sell first to the second-tier companies—the largest are too embroiled in their legacy systems. In this early stage, we need to focus our Customer Experience on that early awareness, and we will use our website and some case studies of early adopters to showcase events to influence peer groups and get the independent consultants up to speed. We shall drive customers to our

website, so we need to make sure that experience is the best. We need clear, simple navigation. We need a clean separation of functional dialog and technical dialog.

While it is best if the Customer Experience aspect is ingrained in the process, in the early days it may be useful to have an individual whose job is to act as the advocate for Customer Experience. As the sales/marketing strategy is developed, a separate person—the CE guy—needs to insist that the team runs through the experience that the customer will have through all stages of the life cycle.

> Let's think through the access to the website. The customer hears about us and our linkage to the product category. What will he/she do when reaching the home page? Will he/she key in the category to search? Will he/she try to find the category under our banner heading "Products and Services"? Will either of these take him/her to the page description? On that page, will a video do a better job than a written description?

Always consider and debate trade-offs. In the example above, what will it cost to make the video? Is that a better use of resources than other options?

Developing product strategy and tactics

There is significant variety in how companies develop their product strategy (longer term) and tactics (shorter term). However, there are several common elements, including the use of the Business Model Framework that we set out in Chapter 5.

It is key to clearly define the target marketplace and fully understand their behaviors, attitudes, wants, and needs (BAWN). As part of the exercise, you should determine the customer roles and their importance relative to CE and then develop the touch points relative to the product life cycle.

CE goals should be established using customer-based parameters (e.g., in the awareness phase, a goal might be that within six months, 60% of the target market is at least somewhat aware of the product category and links the vendor to the category). You may also wish to segment this goal to target this awareness level with 80% of Tier 1 customers.

A more formal approach

The CE framework can also be more formally introduced to the process, relating the importance of the various aspects of touch point, role, product life cycle, and customer journey.

This framework, which we call the CE Intersect Chart, is assembled using primary market research methods (see Chapter 14). The matrix below shows an example of this.

Product:	Integrated Widget Mk 6
Stage in Life Cycle	Maturity
Major parts of the Customer Journey	Information gathering and analysis
	Vendor consideration
	Decision and purchase
	Delivery and implementation
	Use

Roles ------------------------>

Touch points	CIO	Head of IT	Procurement	Users	Line of Business Managers	Finance	Legal
Product / service	76%	95%	100%	100%	95%	0%	0%
Customer support	80%	95%	0%	100%	93%	0%	0%
Product documentation	10%	83%	0%	95%	71%	0%	0%
Education programs	5%	71%	5%	95%	67%	0%	0%
Peer views	98%	61%	54%	63%	64%	0%	0%
Emails	3%	60%	5%	45%	67%	0%	0%
Vendor proposal	65%	60%	100%	35%	68%	100%	100%
Sales staff	29%	59%	95%	12%	62%	100%	100%
Website	10%	57%	2%	90%	59%	0%	0%
Consultant opinion e.g., Gartner	95%	53%	74%	78%	51%	0%	0%
White papers	62%	44%	5%	90%	33%	0%	0%
PR	95%	34%	0%	45%	40%	0%	0%
Press articles / news programs	22%	28%	4%	79%	31%	0%	0%
Advertisements – web, print, TV	10%	23%	2%	21%	21%	0%	0%
Blogs	2%	19%	1%	79%	8%	0%	0%
Press interviews with vendor mgmt.	75%	18%	1%	16%	17%	0%	0%
Social networks	5%	16%	1%	16%	17%	0%	0%
Overall Importance Weight	12%	19%	10%	12%	20%	19%	8%

In this example, with the CFO having a high overall importance weight (19% of the total), the importance of an outstanding proposal and sales staff is very clear. Messages relating to the head of IT need to focus on the product and customer support. Possible resources devoted to social networks would be better used in the more important areas.

PART 3:

The CE Framework

Before beginning implementation of the CEP, an essential element is the planning of the framework within which measurement, action, and feedback will be made.

The framework is the backbone of the CEP, but it also is applicable to successful management of the vendor organization. It comprises the glue that will bring together the strategy at corporate and product level and match this to the customer, the customer sets, customer roles, touch points, product categories, and the customer journey.

7: A HOLISTIC VIEW OF THE CUSTOMER

Understanding your customers and your relationships with them is fundamental to a company's success.

The Apple approach of "build the (best) field and they will come" works well for them, but Apple is a unique sort of company. Most companies need to assert leadership of their customers but also **understand what they want, what they value, and what their behaviors will be. Ron Johnson believed he** could apply the Apple experience to J.C. Penney. The customers did not go for it.

There are two aspects of understanding customers:

- Individually – so that we can track specific individuals and companies over time and provide reactions to their issues
- Aggregated – the accumulation of information about customers as a whole or split between segments or customer sets, which allows broader responses and incorporation into strategy and tactics

If the CE team comes from a market research background, they will likely think more in terms of the aggregated data than individual, whereas both are important. If the team has more of a sales background, they will likely think primarily in terms of individual.

Individual customer data

The holistic view of an individual customer will come from a lot of sources:

- Vendor's financial data
    - What they buy, how much, and how frequently? What is the overall margin associated with their mix of purchases? Are they increasing or decreasing their spend? What is their payment history? How much do they spend with our competitors?
- Demographic data
    - How large is the customer? Which industry? Credit worthiness? Location?
- Customer-facing staff
    - What do the sales people say about each customer?
    - Services people?
    - Channel partners?
    - Executives?
- Market research
    - Wants and needs
    - Behaviors, values, and attitudes
    - Brand image
    - Decision-making structure and process
    - Competitive
    - Satisfaction
        - Transactions
        - Relationship
        - Loyalty

Executives often (and rightly) visit some of the largest customers. Executives are smart and often get to the real issues, but on many occasions, the individuals they meet have been set up by the sales representative so that there is typically a "sunny side up" aspect to the meetings. In addition, visiting just the largest may provide a biased view for the aggregate.

In one case, a computer company executive visited a large insurance company and was told of their needs for an image-processing product. The executive rushed back and had his engineers meet with the customer and develop a new product around their requirements. This more than satisfied the customer, but the product design was based only on that one customer and failed in the broader marketplace.

The scary truth about knowledge of the customer

Anyone would think that major, global companies have a good understanding of their customers. In reality they do not. In fact, many are hard-pressed to even identify the companies they sell to and, even worse, identify the people within the customer organization who are buying or influencing buying decisions. One of the major difficulties at the measurement stage is acquiring a sound sample of customer individuals to interview.

Often the names will come from a CRM system, but just as often the salespeople responsible for input to the system want to guard their contacts from abuse (e.g., marketing emails, requests for interviews, etc.) while also maintaining leverage over client ownership. The contact information is often incomplete or has been entered incorrectly (e.g., an email address without the "@"). Salespeople are remunerated to sell, not to be perfect in their administration, so even the most sophisticated companies tolerate poor information in their CRM systems.

Another use of the view of the customer comes from a need to know which customers are generating a certain level of the vendor's revenue. Well, that sounds easy! Not so in reality. Despite the need, the maintenance of customer databases is usually regarded as a "nonessential" cost until a senior executive wants to make a decision and the information is either not available or thought to be of suspect quality.

We have not seen it in action, but there is an argument for the CEP team to manage the various databases and their interaction and to have the budget and staffing that will allow that to happen. Nevertheless, if a CEO sees the value, he/she can make it happen.

> One software company CEO believed that their success was driven, to a large extent, by their customer database/CRM system. In this case, a fundamental aspect of the remuneration and goal system for the sales force was the quality of customer data and the sales representative's identification and input (by the sales team) of an accurate Net Promoter Score (NPS). An independent market research-based survey verified the scores, but sales management insisted that sales representatives justify any variation. There was also a process in place to drive the NPS higher in individual customers who had low scores. It became a fundamental part of account management. Safeguards were also put in place to restrict overuse of the contact information in terms of ad hoc surveys, telemarketing campaigns, etc.

Aggregated data
While "individual" data is used to react to issues raised by specific customers, aggregated data is necessary for addressing more systemic problems or opportunities. Most vendors cannot/do not develop and sell unique products for each individual customer. They provide quantities of product that will satisfy the needs of many. The Customer Experience must be superior across the customer base, and vendors need to understand these aggregated needs to best implement their CE strategies.

Some people call this the "voice of the customer," which is often just a technique for capturing a customer's behaviors, attitudes, needs, and wants. If data on individual customers has been captured in a structured format, aggregation is straightforward.

There is a wide range of other approaches to gathering this data: focus groups, in-depth approaches (loosely structured interviews), quantitative interviews through web surveys or telephone surveys, ethnographic approaches (such as follow-home), web-based behavioral approaches (e.g., observing interaction with a website), and many others. The approaches are basic market research methodologies and can use a non-identified set of customers (and prospects). Data is provided at the aggregate level and rarely at the individual level.

Segmentation of customers
Aggregated data can be used across a vendor's customers. The magical "average" can be used to net out the aberrations found at an individual level. Thus we might have a finding that tells us that customers, on average, award us a 53 NPS, but this "one size fits all" mentality can be flawed. This is the average across all customers, probably assuming that each is equal to any other. The average NPS of our largest customers may be significantly lower, which could result in making some incorrect decisions.

Part of our holistic view of the customer is to view them in logical segments, which enables us to view the characteristics of different sets of customers.

The hallmarks of a good segmentation are:

1. Within each segment, the characteristics of its members should be similar: they should behave the same; they should have similar attitudes, wants, and needs.
2. Between segments, the characteristics of the members should be different: they should behave differently; they should have different characteristics.
3. The segments should be generally equal in size—no one segment dominates dramatically.
4. The numbers of customers and their market size in each segment must be able to be measured.
5. The segmentation must be stable over a reasonable time period—three to five years.

6. Any customer should be able to be allocated easily to a segment.
7. The number of segments should be manageable—fewer than eight.

Segmentation allows development and implementation of different strategies to target the customers' needs and wants using the touch points that work best.

There are four types of segmentation:

- Administrative – a well-defined category such as country: "The customer is headquartered in Germany."
- Behavioral/attitudinal – those customers with similar behaviors/attitudes
- Wants/needs – those with common wants/needs
- Retention/targeting – identification of "at risk" groups of customers vs. "loyal" customers

The most common segmentation used is **administrative**—geography, industry, size of company—but this often fails on our criteria of good segmentation. While many vendors organize their sales force by country and industry, the real difference between these groupings is often small. The use of industry-specialized software is appropriate for a specific industry, but this equates to just one segment. Selling computer hardware is similar in every industry, and in the present day, buying behavior does not shift much regardless of whether the customer is in Vietnam or Germany. Administrative segmentation is great for classification but little else.

Behavioral and attitudinal (and wants and needs) segmentation creates problems in classification. You cannot look up a company in Dun and Bradstreet and see that they are a "technocrat," whereas you can determine that they are a midsize engineering company in Oklahoma. However, if the segmentation work has been undertaken well, it will score well on the other "good segmentation" criteria. While the categorization is difficult, it can be achieved on a customer-by-customer basis and become an asset that cannot easily be duplicated by competitors.

Somewhat like CE, segmentation has enormous potential value but is not easy to implement. The mechanical aspects of the research to develop it are straightforward, but the real value comes from its acceptance and then the actions that are necessary.

One major program that we have worked on is set out below to show the post-research aspects of the approach.

> An initial buyer behavior/attitude study was undertaken by McKinsey and Co., and this was followed up by a broader study by RONIN. In that study, in-depth interviews were undertaken as a prelude to a quantitative study across the United States, Europe, and Japan.

> Out of this emerged a segmentation that satisfied all the criteria set out above, but identifying a specific customer to a segment required answering four straightforward questions. While an administrative segmentation could have allocated customers based on publically available data (e.g., SIC code), this approach required more effort but also provided a competitive advantage since other vendors could not replicate the approach easily.

> The segmentation explained a lot of aspects that had previously been mysteries. A set of three savings banks in the south of Germany had identical demographics but behaved fundamentally differently. The segmentation showed their characteristics of behavior were linked to their segment and that they behaved the same as companies in the same segment in other industries, across other countries, and across other size classes.

> Another aspect was the distribution of the revenue opportunity. One particular segment was small in most countries but very large in Japan. It was

in this segment where our client had least penetration. The product set, the sales approach, and the marketing approaches had been developed intuitively in the United States and did not apply to this large segment in Japan.

Our client embraced the segmentation and, over the course of the next two years, built much of its product development, marketing, and sales around the segmentation. To support this, we trained over 1,000 people in the segmentation, and conducted 42 strategy workshops using the segmentation criteria to be used in messaging, value propositions, advertising, and marketing materials.

Other efforts involved an online calculator, which allowed sales staff to answer the four questions for their customers and be led in product selection, positioning, and sales messages.

Two country organizations implemented the approach in their inbound call centers so that when customers called in, they would be asked the four questions and then categorized, and thereafter relevant messaging would be used in discussions at the sales and support levels.

While never quantified, the effort was regarded as a huge success and was driven by a group executive who instilled the approach in everyone he met, changing the culture to match this new approach.

His success led to his promotion. His successor did not have the same passion, and use of the segmentation eroded over time.

In a second study, we found a marketplace that was bifurcated.

In a five-year research program of IT decision makers, RONIN developed a segmentation around the fundamental approach that the company was taking toward the dynamic economic climate. We asked IT decision makers to answer the following question:

Which of the following best describes your company's actions under the current economic conditions?

1. We are taking a very short-term view, concentrating on cost reduction and postponing more strategic actions.
2. We are undertaking a number of strategic initiatives to be more competitive.

We then separated the data into two sets—one for "short termers" (response 1) and one for "strategics" (response 2). Interestingly, each segment contained about 50% of the respondents. And each data set had fundamentally different characteristics from the other but was internally consistent. It was clear that the marketplace was bifurcated.

If we look at the marketplace as a whole, we can get it wrong. On a 1-7 scale the "strategics" might say "7" and the "short termers" might say "1." Without separation we reach an average of "4," which is not very useful; acting on this could match none of the marketplace needs.

Retention/targeting segmentation
In many industries, particularly if the markets are mature, the issue of retention of customers is paramount. A mature market has low growth and is highly competitive with a trend toward commoditization of the product set. Gains for a vendor come primarily by having customers switch from a competitor to you.

We have observed there can be switching (in which one vendor is dropped and another takes its place) or shifting (where some of the business is shifted from one vendor to another, though not all of it).

In retention/targeting, the vendor tags each of its customers so as to determine the "at risk" situations and to also determine where the vendor has presence in the account but not all the business. Similarly, if the vendor has a database of prospects who are candidates for possible switching, a tag should be added to determine the most vulnerable competitor accounts.

The tag should indicate:

- Risk of switching
- Risk of shifting (the percentage of spend shifting from us to a competitor)
- If the customer is at high risk of canceling the company's service
- Value of the customer—amount of spend, profitability of account—which indicates how much effort is justified to retain the account

For at-risk but valuable customers, the vendor needs to develop tactics to retain these (e.g., dedicated account team, better delivery times/methods, and education). This is just like any other segmentation schema; it is used to develop ways of improving the Customer Experience that may be different for other segments.

A similar approach is used for targeting competitive accounts.

Customer sets

Segmentation is determined by the marketplace; each segment has a number of members with common characteristics. In determining the groups of customers that will be analyzed in the CEP—which we shall call "customer sets"—the criteria is often different, relating more toward an administrative segmentation such as Tier 1, Tier 2, Tier 3 customers and perhaps based on their level of spend. This is covered in detail in Chapter 8.

Customer identification

There can be a lot of confusion when dealing with customer groups, particularly within large corporations. These are held together in a complex structure with different subsidiaries, divisions, and geographic units.

Your sales organization structure does not necessarily reflect the customer structure.

Most vendors establish customer numbers and use these in their CRM systems. Frequently this does not serve the vendor well. In large customers (probably the ones you really are interested in) there can be many buying units across business units, across countries, etc., and frequently the vendor customer number does not allow the necessary linkages. In addition, there is no way to link external data to a customer record.

While the Dun and Bradstreet structure is not perfect, it is an excellent way to structure corporations on a global scale.

D&B splits enterprises into three groupings:

- Global ultimate – e.g., Ford Motor Corporation
- Country – e.g., Ford Germany
- Establishment – e.g., a distribution center in Munich

A regional headquarters (e.g., Ford Europe) would be an establishment in a country (e.g., Ford Europe HQ is an establishment in Cologne, Germany).

While this does not address the different decision-making units in business units located in one physical location, it is better than nothing.

This structure can be used for a variety of purposes. It can be used for market sizing and market analysis.

There is also a significant amount of demographic information that can be attached to the customer record.

A single customer database?

Clearly, a single (logical) database containing all the data about each customer is highly desirable. Often the CRM system is thought to be the logical place to keep this, but a vendor's current CRM systems are typically configured with a much more limited functionality.

The database needs to allow a hierarchy of access as well. Certain financial data about a customer may be restricted so that individuals on the account team do not have access to it. The CE index, however, is something that should be on the system and widely available.

It is better to have a separate customer access portal that links to multiple databases and allows individuals to view and/or update it, based on access rights. An identifier needs to be in place to allow this linkage; the most commonly used is the D&B number, which also allows access to external data.

The customer database will provide the individual customer information and become the basis for segmentation and aggregated data analysis.

8: CUSTOMER SETS

The next aspect is to determine customer sets.

As set out above, we do not want to treat every customer equally. The smaller customers (and there will be a lot more of these) will skew the data if we look just at averages, and if there are significant differences in different customer sets, an average can be very misleading.

In addition, problems that come to light at an individual customer level will usually be addressed differently. If one of the largest customers is unhappy, we shall bend over backwards to rectify the situation. If a very small customer is unhappy, we might apply a different approach.

Developing customer sets is most commonly done based on size of the account. The simplest approach is to use the revenue from each account to place each into the Tier 1, 2, or 3 groupings.

Care needs to be taken, though, so that we do not use just this measure.

> In a classic case, the previous year's revenue from each customer was used, and this resulted in dropping several accounts which had been Tier 1 to Tier 2 and provided them with no account team. We found that the shortfall in revenue was driven by a life cycle issue and that when

the vendor thought they were less important and reduced coverage, they were wooed and finally won by a competitor.

A smarter approach has been to consider opportunity and view customers over a longer time frame.

Indeed, one on line brokerage we worked with used a combination of revenue and growth over time to pick out its "platinum" accounts.

Another aspect is to determine how prospects are to be included. Some of these could have a very large potential, which is going to competitors at present. Others have a low potential. It is sensible to separate these and not just put them into a pool of "competitive accounts."

Another aspect of the customer set as it relates to CE is the profitability of different accounts. It is now clear that the largest companies (who probably are the largest customers in terms of sales value) have often negotiated discounting and other terms that make the margin on these sales lower than the next tier. Some vendors are now using the net margin or account profitability to determine the tiers rather than sales value.

Often the customer set tiering is aligned with sales coverage. For Tier 1, the coverage is by dedicated account teams; for Tier 2, a shared direct sales group; and for Tier 3, use of indirect channels. For a sales organization this is appropriate, but for Customer Experience and multichannel touch points, a larger set may be of more value and would be easy enough to implement. These will probably be subsets of the sales organization tiering.

For CE as well, it can be extremely valuable to use customer segmentation approaches to split the tiers.

Following is an example of ten customers and the parameters that might determine their tier.

	Revenue past year	Margin past year	Revenue past three years	Margin past three years	Total spend past year	Total spend past three years
Customer A	5	1	25	4	8	37
Customer B	2	1	20	8	4	12
Customer C	3	1	15	2	6	45
Customer D	10	1	30	0	50	180
Customer E	13	2	28	0	26	84
Customer F	6	1	12	0	24	60
Customer G	9	2	21	0	54	126
Customer H	6	2	20	0	24	100
Customer I	7	1	14	0	63	126
Customer J	11	2	26	0	121	78

In allocating these to tiers, if we used just this year's revenue, customers E, J, and D would logically be in Tier 1. However, using margin for the past year finds a different set—G and I as well as E and J. Viewing the revenue over the past three years catapults A into Tier 1. If we look at the customer's total spend (on us and our competitors), another set of customers become the most attractive. Which criteria should we use?

There is no right answer, and it will depend partly on your sales strategy. If you are concentrating on maintaining your own base, the total spend metric will be less important except to alert you to areas of vulnerability. If your products are typically purchased in cycles, with one year being high and the next low, it does not make sense to make the sales from last year the criterion for this year's tiering. What makes most sense is to carry all this information in the customer database and use it for analysis. Do we have a low CE score when we have little share of the account's total spend?

9: CUSTOMER ROLES

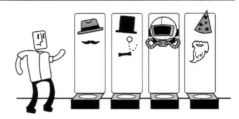

A CRM system is probably better called a "sales contact" database. Most implementations are geared to the sales force and provide a consistent repository into which the sales representative enters (and keeps up-to-date?) their customers' and prospects' contact details with some notes to help the sales process. Rarely does the database contain the names and contact details of individuals other than the main sales contact. Thus, when we consider the Customer Experience as including all individuals who experience the vendor and its product set, we are missing the end users, the people in purchasing, the legal team, executive management (who might also have a veto power), the CFO, etc. The CEP needs to address all individuals who are in contact with the vendor and its products through the entire life cycle of the products and not just at the lead-up to a sale.

The relevant roles in the customer organization will need to be custom developed for each individual CEP. For some product sets, the importance of the Customer Experience to some roles will be very different from that in others. This will also vary a lot by customer (e.g., in one, the purchasing group may have little impact, and if they are upset because of the way they are treated, it may not in any way affect the relationship). In other companies, the purchasing group may have a right of veto, which makes them much more important in the relationship.

For the Tier 1 customers, decisions regarding important roles can best be made by the account teams (if you have these). Ideally this is recorded in the CRM system and provides the individuals that will be surveyed. However, you should use some other methods to check these. The sales team will be interested primarily in selling (as they should be!) and may not be aware of the user community or higher-level executives who might be critical for the longer-term relationship.

For the Tier 2 and lower, the CEP team, perhaps with the help of the sales-people, should develop the likely important role categories.

A more systematic approach would involve in-depth interviews with a number of customers in the non-Tier 1 accounts.

However, the most useful approach that we have found is to ask, through a quantitative survey with the main decision maker, the importance of these different roles. The questions need to be asked in the context of the different product categories (e.g., we found that marketing management had an important role in a computer-based analytics package, whereas that had no role in other software that the vendor was selling). When the important roles have been identified, the research program needs to address these and not just the main decision maker.

Think through the total life cycle for the category from awareness to usage over time. Who is involved at each stage? How important are they?

> In a discussion with the CIO of one of the largest United States banks, he made it clear that their legal people had vetoed a number of small/ midsized vendors because they lacked the legal teams necessary to ne-gotiate the onerous contractual terms that the bank required. The sales team did not even know the legal people were involved.

Customer roles developed for one IT "branch office software" client were:

- CEO
- CFO
- CIO
- Head of IT
- Head of data center
- Legal
- Purchasing
- Branch office management

Prioritization of roles

If we collect data from, say, 20 people in a customer organization across the various roles, do we take just a simple average of their scores and use that in our analysis? Clearly some individuals are more important than others. One method we have used to assess this is to ask each individual to list the hierarchy of importance in the "customer wide experience." Then we used this aggregated data to weight the answers. We found a reasonable consensus across the various players.

10: TOUCH POINTS

Touch points are the interfaces between the vendor and the customer, and there are a wide range of these that will fashion the Customer Experience.

Many programs ignore this diversity and ask just about the overall experience. This may be fine in some situations but may not give you the granularity that you need for influencing action.

What are the touch points?

The touch points include both those in the vendor's control and those that can only be influenced. The need is to develop and define these categories and then understand the importance of these as well as how well the customer rates the vendor on each of them.

Controlled touch points include:

- Product/service
  - Does it meet the basic wants and needs of the customer (threshold)?
  - Is it easy to buy, implement, and use?

- How does it match up to competitive products?
- Sales staff
  - Are they knowledgeable?
  - Are they helpful?
  - Are they nice to know?
- Website
  - Is it easy to find the information needed? Often this is poor, particularly if a large company has a very diverse product set and a lot of business units that provide a siloed approach.
  - Do you understand what is being said? There can be problems related to vendor-speak (e.g., "select the product number that you are interested in").
- Emails
  - These can be really bad (e.g., "Hi BUNN, HARRY"), and if they are too frequent, they can annoy and/or cause the customer to filter them to a spam folder.
- Social networks
  - This is the "soup de jour," but it must be handled very carefully. In a study we undertook recently, we found that most B2B decision makers do not use social media for business-related information or to aid their decision making.
- Advertisements – web, print, TV
  - Are these actually passé in this information-rich age? They may be attention-getting, but do they really convey your message better than more information-oriented collateral? Maybe they work in B2C, but they have little value to B2B buyers. Corporate ads have little value in the Customer Experience other than establishing financial strength/credibility.
- PR
  - This can be powerful but works best if the releases align with the customer and are more informative than just sales pitches.

- Interviews
  - Because short videos are easy to implement, a simple collection of short videos (Q&A sessions, etc.) can be a great touch point.
- Customer support
  - The customer support function is fundamental but is too often budget-squeezed, and the service poor. This is probably the most important touch point. If a customer needs help, can they get it accurately, easily, and enjoyably?
- Education programs
  - For complex products, education programs can be very important. Many years ago, IBM had their Customer Education Program as part of their marketing budget and provided it free of charge.
- Instruction aids
  - Steve Jobs was driven to make Apple products "manual-free." In the book *Steve Jobs* by Walter Isaacson, he is described as being driven by the Atari arcade game that simply stated, "Insert quarter. Avoid Klingons." The shift to intuitive operation in B2C products has come a long way. No longer does the consumer need to put up with the flashing 12:00 on their TV set when setting the time is a complex operation. No longer does a "point and shoot" camera vendor need to supply a thick manual. And now the newer B2B products are embracing this approach. There is, however, an assumption of knowledge by the customer, and this needs to be explored before going too far down this path. It will affect the post-sale/use phases of the Customer Experience.
- White papers
  - White papers are very powerful but must go beyond a sales pitch, such as "how the Model 544E solved the problem."
- Vendor-sponsored events
  - These can be mediocre based on "one size fits all," packaged PowerPoint presentations. Customizing these requires more resources but can make an important impact on the Customer Experience, particularly in one-on-one meetings.

Uncontrolled touch points include:

- Peer views
  - Online has become more important than "word of mouth."
- Press articles/news programs
- Blogs
- Consultant opinion, e.g., Gartner, Forrester

Social media as a touch point

There has been so much hype about social media in recent years, it seems that few organizations can afford to stand by and watch it all unfold. So is social media on every organization's radar by now? According to our most recent global technology Pulse survey, the answer is no—at least not yet:

- 43% of organizations worldwide have <u>not</u> used social media for business purposes.
- 54% have a presence on third-party social media sites.
- 33% do microblog (e.g., tweets).
- 31% publish blogs targeted at their customers and prospects.
- 25% include social sharing buttons in emails and web offers.
- 23% build applications/widgets on social media sites.
- 22% run company-hosted communities.

Most organizations use social media to increase awareness, engage customers, cultivate promoters, and generate leads. Social media's effectiveness is shown primarily in increasing awareness and customer involvement, not in converting sales. The emphasis has been put on getting people involved and keeping them involved. Using social networks to socialize may be easy, but turning all that socializing into cash flow still eludes most organizations.

In a B2B setting, getting sales from social media is even more difficult that it is in a B2C company because the purchase decision-making process is far more complex, and decisions usually involve multiple people in an organization.

Nevertheless, social media can be valuable to B2B organizations when it comes to cultivating a strong relationship. Since the CE index has a high correlation with purchases, it is an important bridge to cross. B2B social media marketing can help nurture promoters and spread the influence in three important ways:

- Help customers share their best experiences, champion your company, and endorse your offerings. These can be reviews on third-party sites, the responses to queries on LinkedIn groups or Twitter, the posts shared on your own community, etc.
- Build a strong thought leadership through blogging. With social media, you can build connections without the need to get past gatekeepers such as editors. A highly resonant blog will earn you trust and respect from your customers and prospects, and an active, engaged audience is a strong marketing asset in itself.
- Leverage social media to improve SEO. Roughly one-third of all commercial searches on Google are B2B in nature, more than 50% of Google's target advertisers are B2B, and almost 38% of Yahoo's target advertisers are B2B. Clearly, SEO is essential for B2B marketers to succeed. The more frequently your content is shared on social media, the more likely you will get ahead in organic searches.

Defining the appropriate touch points

In each vendor situation the touch points that are most important will differ. Defining the appropriate touch points is based on strategy/positioning:

- If your product set is largely mature, concentrate on end steps of the customer journey.
- If your strategic positioning is "ease of use," design aspects are more important than customer service, and the vendor needs to make the touch points appropriate

In some cases value can be gained by splitting the main touch point categories to allow greater actionability (e.g., within customer service, explore the IVR system, waiting times, representative manner, representative knowledge, etc.).

RONIN undertakes research of the IT marketplace globally, which we call the Pulse Program. In a recent wave of the study, we asked 1,200 IT decision makers what touch points were the most important in their experience with their primary IT vendor.

On average, they chose just eight out of our list of 16. The chart below shows the percentages that gave a high importance score to each.

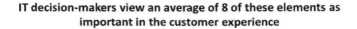

IT decision-makers view an average of 8 of these elements as important in the customer experience

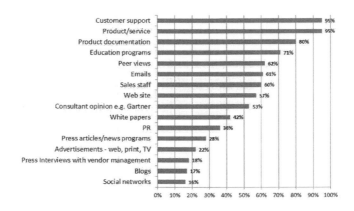

The first two were expected, but the next two were a surprise. Only 16% of the decision makers regarded social networks as an important touch point.

We then asked them to rate the experience in each. This allowed us to match the importance with the rating.

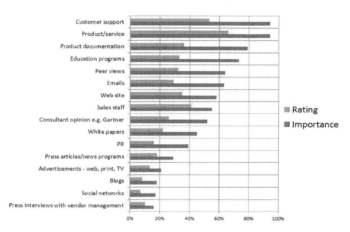

Looking at importance and the rating of their primary vendor we see "scope for improvement"

Since no vendor has unlimited resources, it is optimal to do well in the areas that are most important. Getting better at something that no one cares about is a waste.

By subtracting the Rating from the Importance, we developed a gap analysis, and this shows clearly what has to be actioned.

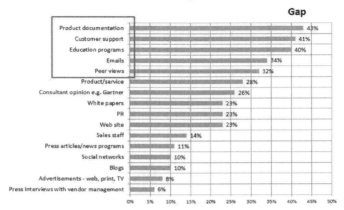

Vendors can gain "biggest bang for the buck" by focusing on the largest gaps between importance and rating

Summing up, the CEP has to establish a set of touch points that are relevant for that vendor and use these in the CEP. The data collection of touch points may be undertaken independently of the data collection of the CE information and used just to establish the priorities.

11: PRODUCT CATEGORIES

I am product manager for the WidgetExpressLite. I need to understand how the Customer Experience is regarded by my customers.

Unfortunately, the "Widget" company has several thousand products, and each customer probably has 20 or 30. How can we possible measure the CE of each without driving the customer and our CE team insane?

The logical approach is to group products and apply the measurements to these groups; a simpler approach is to just measure the overall relationship. This latter approach, however, is like the "average"—it can mask a lot of diversity and may not offer value to the managers with product responsibility.

Collecting CE data at a product level that provides the optimal value in terms of both individual action and aggregated analysis can be challenging. The product category set selected must also be matched with information in the customer database so that valid customers can be surveyed and so that supporting analysis is possible. The customer set profile must be held in the customer database.

In addition, each product will likely be at a different stage in its life cycle; therefore each will have a different set of associated roles and relevant touch points. For example, if a product is at the early awareness stage, legal, finance, and purchasing are unlikely to be involved, and the main touch points will be oriented to education (e.g., whitepapers, webinars, conferences, etc.). A product at the end of the maturity stage will involve purchasing and the user community more and will be related to use rather than awareness or purchase. Although we have not observed it, grouping by stage in life cycle and focusing on customer journey and touch points might be a very effective categorization approach.

At the end of the day, you need categories that will allow a sufficient number of completed customer surveys for valid analysis—you need to be able to "slice and dice." The questionnaire must, however, enable you to find out whether customers with a low score are driven by their experience with a specific product set or whether it is more a measurement of the overall relationship.

Consequently, the CEP is not just a measurement exercise, but one that identifies issues at a level where actions can be taken.

The key is to determine what the categories will be and then publish them. What often happens is that the program is set up with unclear categories, and the results are then muddled and expectations are not met. The first attempt at these is unlikely to be the perfect solution, but decisions have to be made. The framework must allow changes over time.

12: CUSTOMER JOURNEY AND THE LIFE CYCLE PORTFOLIO

The customer journey and the product life cycle are two separate but linked aspects that are fundamental to the development of your CEP.

Customer journey

For each product or service, individual customers take a "journey" from early awareness of the product category and the way this type of product can satisfy their needs, to end of life when the product has been used and finally retired to make way for something newer. The journey passes through a number of phases, an example of which is set out below:

The Customer Experience is a Journey

- Category awareness
- Product/service awareness
- Information gathering and analysis
- Vendor consideration
- Decision and purchase
- Delivery and implementation
- Use
- Retain

The steps in the customer journey will vary for each vendor. The set shown above was used for a specific set of IT products.

Each step has its own set of roles and optimal touch points. For example, for an IT application, the information gathering and analysis will likely involve technical staff in the IT department as well as members of the end-user group. Access to the vendor's website will be complemented by access to research analyst reports (e.g., Gartner, Forrester) and also advice from external consultants. At the "Use" step, only "users" are involved, and their touch points will relate to the product itself as well as customer support on the web and in customer support telephone calls.

In developing the product strategy and tactics, each step in the customer journey is laid out, and the relevant roles and touch points developed and documented.

Depending on the strategy, a vendor may have some of the steps broken down in more detail.

In one software company, the strategic positioning was around customer service, so three steps in the customer journey related to aspects of this.

Product life cycle

The product life cycle needs to be overlaid on the customer journey.

All new customers will take the customer journey. Even if the product is well established in the marketplace (and the customer is a late adopter), they will still take the full journey—albeit more rapidly and with less rigor. Thus the early customer journey steps in a mature market will be easily understood and well documented, whereas in an embryonic marketplace they will need greater research and proof points.

If the product focus is on new customers within a mature marketplace, the relevant roles and touch points will be different than if the mature marketplace is being addressed as a whole.

The framework for the CEP and the holistic view required for the customer varies with each stage as is set out below:

Firstly, all products and services travel through a life cycle from their initial inception to when they are replaced by newer offerings. A major part of a vendor's corporate strategy is to develop a portfolio of products that allows profitable and sustainable growth over time. There needs to be a percentage of products in the maturity phase to allow solid profitability, but as these slow in growth, there has to be another set of products that are in the embryonic and growth phases. These will provide profit and growth going forward. The Customer Experience is different at each stage: In the early days, the experience of finding out about the category and the vendors who have early products is most important. In the "decline" stage, the experience of maintenance for installed products is the main thrust. The touch points will be different, as will the needs, wants, and expectations. The importance of various roles will also be different.

The market planning process is typically in place to guide the process across time through the various phases:

Embryonic – What should we develop? What needs will drive demand? What features will differentiate it? What volume can we sell? What should the price point be?

Introduction – Who will be the first buyers? How do we get them to pioneer the offering?

Growth – How do we cross the chasm from embryonic to the growth stage?

Maturity – How do we sell competitively when the need and offering are well understood and accepted?

Decline – When should we exit? What should the midlife kickers be? What have we learned to allow the next generation to succeed?

Each product grouping can have a different customer journey that matches in detail the path through the life cycle. One step in setting up the framework is to develop the set of life-cycle steps that are most useful in your arena.

Development of the customer journey

Developing the customer journey is an important aspect of Customer Experience. It also translates directly into the corporate and product line strategies. It is not just an aspect of CE measurement.

So how do we develop it?

1: Strategic review

This is a high-level review of the corporate and product line strategies to determine the focus in these areas:

- Are we focused on just our existing customers? How does competitive account switching play?
- What is our product portfolio in terms of life cycle? Which life cycle phase is most important?
- What customer sets have we decided on? How are these different from one another?
- What are the wants and needs of our target market? This comes from our holistic view of the customer held in our customer database.

This set of insights are summarized and used as input to a strategic workshop in Step 3 below.

2: Field staff input on the customer journey

The field staff—sales representatives, service engineers, and the like—have a sound understanding of the customer journey, and it would be foolish to ignore them. In-depth interviews with some of these people should be conducted, to discuss this basic point: "Walk me through the steps of how a customer interfaces with us from becoming aware of the product category to end of life."

Information on the touch points they use and the customer roles who will be involved will also emerge from these interviews.

3: Straw man workshop

The inputs from 1 and 2 are then used to develop a straw man of the customer journey. It will include the steps that are most relevant; the structure should not have more than 12 steps.

For each step in the customer journey, the team should develop the questions that the customer will want answered and how they will judge success. For example, if there is an "Information Gathering" step, they may want to understand how the product would work in their current infrastructure, what ROI might be expected, and what a ballpark cost might be.

The relevant touch points and customer roles for each would also be discussed and recorded.

Out of this, a straw man of the customer journey will be developed.

4: In-depth interviews with customers

The straw man will have been developed internally in the vendor organization and needs to be tested with customers. The in-depth interviews should be with individuals in a few of the roles, and the discussion should center on whether the customer journey steps are all-embracing and nothing has been left out. The customer may not see the value of some of the detailed steps (e.g., in our customer service emphasis example) but that is not a problem. If we have omitted steps, it is a problem.

In the same interviews, we explore the relevant touch points in each step as well as the customer roles.

It is important to include customers from each of our tiers.

The output from this study allows the straw man to be adjusted and becomes the basis for a quantitative study.

5: Quantitative study

This is a broad study including both customers and noncustomers. It tests the updated straw man with a much larger buyer set. It also gathers information on the importance of touch points and roles against each of the steps in the customer journey.

6: Life cycle overlay

The overall life cycle of each customer set and product category is overlaid on the customer journey study results.

7: Customer Experience intersect charts

The data is developed into a series of charts showing the intersection of:

- Product category
- Customer set
- Stage in life cycle
- Step in customer journey
- Customer roles
- Touch points

Some aspects can be collapsed for simplicity.

The chart below shows an example:

	Product:	Integrated Widget Mk 6					
	Stage in Life Cycle	Maturity					
Major parts of the Customer Journey		Information gathering and analysis					
		Vendor consideration					
		Decision and purchase					
		Delivery and implementation					
		Use					

| | Roles ------------------------------> | | | | Line of Business | | |
Touch points	CIO	Head of IT	Procurement	Users	Managers	Finance	Legal
Product / service	76%	95%	100%	100%	95%	0%	0%
Customer support	80%	95%	0%	100%	93%	0%	0%
Product documentation	10%	83%	0%	95%	71%	0%	0%
Education programs	5%	71%	5%	95%	67%	0%	0%
Peer views	98%	61%	54%	63%	64%	0%	0%
Emails	3%	60%	5%	45%	67%	0%	0%
Vendor proposal	65%	60%	100%	35%	68%	100%	100%
Sales staff	29%	59%	95%	12%	62%	100%	100%
Website	10%	57%	2%	90%	59%	0%	0%
Consultant opinion e.g., Gartner	95%	53%	74%	78%	51%	0%	0%
White papers	62%	44%	5%	90%	33%	0%	0%
PR	95%	34%	0%	45%	40%	0%	0%
Press articles / news programs	22%	28%	4%	79%	31%	0%	0%
Advertisements – web, print, TV	10%	23%	2%	21%	21%	0%	0%
Blogs	2%	19%	1%	79%	8%	0%	0%
Press interviews with vendor mgmt.	75%	18%	1%	16%	17%	0%	0%
Social networks	5%	16%	1%	16%	17%	0%	0%
Overall Importance Weight	12%	19%	10%	12%	20%	19%	8%

PART 4:

Implementation

When the framework has been established, it is time to implement the program. This comprises measurement of the Customer Experience, development of the actions required to improve it, and finally the feedback to the customers that shows we are listening and acting.

13: MEASUREMENT – THE PATH FROM CUSTOMER SATISFACTION TO CE

One, but only one, aspect of the CEP is the "discovery" of how the customers view the vendor. Are they satisfied? Do they feel loyalty? What are their problems with the vendor?

A Customer Experience Program is most commonly seen as an extension of the customer satisfaction program. Often the same players are involved, and unfortunately many CEPs are really nothing more than a renamed customer satisfaction program. Interestingly, sometimes the Customer Experience team has limited market research experience and can make some serious errors in the collection and interpretation of customer data.

Nevertheless, understanding the customer satisfaction roots is important, and ensuring that the base is sound is fundamental to the successful implementation of a CEP.

Let's pause and review customer satisfaction programs.

The flavors of customer satisfaction

B2B customer satisfaction programs can address a variety of aspects of the interface between the vendor and the customer.

Transactional

This is the most common and easiest to implement. The concept here is to ask the customer what his/her experience was with a recent transaction. "You just purchased a dozen computer servers. How was the experience?"

This needs to be continuous during the year and is used as a rapid response to issues, particularly when a systemic problem starts to appear. For example, in one situation it became clear quickly that access to a website for delivery-status checking was not working.

Relationship

This is a broader approach aimed at understanding how the customer feels about the relationship rather than just individual transactions.

Transactional studies are focused and simple and best done immediately following the transaction. Evaluating a customer's relationship with the vendor goes beyond the sum of all individual transactions. It includes every detail of the customer's experience along with all the emotional and branding issues.

In one project we found that the current survey did not explicitly frame the questions around either transactions or relationships, although the sample selection was triggered by transactions. Consequently, there was confusion regarding what the final data meant and how it could be used.

It is important to recognize that assessing a customer's satisfaction with a specific transaction is very different from assessing the quality of a customer relationship.

Most transactions, even if perfectly handled, are not important enough to create a promoter. But a dissatisfied transaction can easily create a detractor.

Our recommendation was to limit the transaction-related satisfaction questions to one or two and then use the majority of the real estate for relationship-driven satisfaction measurement (e.g., considering all aspects of your experience with Vendor X up to this point, how would you rate the experience?).

Loyalty

When asked why his customers were not loyal to the company brand, the head of a major personal computer group famously answered, "If you want loyalty, get a dog."

Satisfaction and loyalty do not necessarily track. In a recent global study of IT decision makers, we asked questions about both—satisfaction and loyalty. The loyalty question included a definition stressing "a feeling of devotion" while the satisfaction question addressed the relationship, not a recent transaction.

One aspect of the vendor/customer relationship relates to **customer satisfaction.**

On a 1-7 scale where 1 is very unsatisfied and 7 is very satisfied, how would you rate your satisfaction level with your primary vendor?

Loyalty is defined as "a feeling of devotion, duty, or attachment to a person or company". There is an implication that the relationship goes beyond that of a "sound business relationship".

On a scale of 1-7 where 1 is very low level of loyalty and 7 is a very high level of loyalty, how would you rate your overall loyalty towards your primary vendor?

This was a public domain study, and the scores have been previously published. While there is some correlation between loyalty and satisfaction, overall the loyalty to an IT vendor is 14 points lower than satisfaction. Perhaps owning a dog is the way to go!

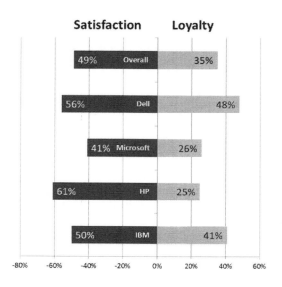

Percentages show "top box" scores – 6 and 7 on the 1-7 scale.

Too often people confuse the two, whereas satisfaction is a behavioral measure and loyalty is attitudinal.

Customer leadership

Loyalty is aligned more with another vendor aspect—customer leadership.

While companies need to "listen to" their customers, they have a responsibility to be leaders of these customers. We have found in customer surveys that while customers can point out problems and "pain points," they tend to think in a fairly short-term way and are unlikely to be innovative in terms of what the vendor can do to avert them.

If a vendor becomes a customer leader, there is a sense of loyalty, but it is more that the customer trusts the vendor, who—even if making mistakes on the way—will get the customer to the optimal point sometime in the future. Leadership implies followers—not those with blind faith, but those who accept and trust that the leader will take them to the right place, albeit with some "bumps in the road."

Customer leadership may be the best measure of true loyalty.

Customer relationship equity

Customer Relationship Equity is a concept we developed for a European telecommunications carrier for their business customers. It matches the level of customer relationship with the value from each account.

> Our client already had a customer segmentation that divided customers into three tiers based on revenue from these accounts. Sales and service resources were organized differently for each group. The largest accounts had a dedicated account team; the Tier 2 accounts had either a single dedicated salesperson or an account team that would operate for several accounts. The Tier 3 level was serviced only through a third-party channel organization.

> Rather than just revenue, the approach we developed used a value score based on the margin of products/services sold into the account and the cost to meet the account's demands. We found that some of the largest accounts negotiated such good deals and were so demanding that the overall profitability of the account was much lower than what a simple revenue number would suggest.

The Customer Relationship Equity approach linked a satisfaction index to the value index. In this case, we found some disturbing disconnects. But we also determined a new set of Tier 1 accounts.

Going forward, this group of high-value customers was flagged, paid special attention to, and then monitored and analyzed separately.

Brand and image

Going beyond customer satisfaction, an important part of the Customer Experience is the relative acceptance of brand fulfillment. This is part of the more emotional aspects of the Customer Experience.

Customers generally associate a brand with a set of values. A well-known and respected brand offers a promise—generally of quality, but also in many cases other attributes that go with the product.

Customers grant their "permission" for specific companies to participate in a product/marketplace. Mac Trucks has the permission of customers to make and sell large trucks. If they released a luxury sedan, they would be unlikely to be successful without a major change of image. In the same way, Jaguar, which has a brand permission to make and sell luxury sedans, would find it difficult to market and sell large trucks.

In our holistic view of the customer, we need to include awareness and preference for specific brands.

Other customer satisfaction programs

As well as the main programs, some specialized programs can be implemented to address such issues as win/loss, post-complaint follow-up, etc. It is important that these are orchestrated under the central customer satisfaction and/or Customer Experience team. This is not to increase the power of the team but to ensure that the customers are not subjected to too many studies.

Competitive

Many years ago, we took over a customer satisfaction program for a computer manufacturer that was aimed at a specific computer brand. The vendor was happy with the previous results as was evidenced by their simple scorecard approach to the results: in the past year they had increased from a B- to a B+. They were not measuring satisfaction with competitive products, and we convinced them to include this in our first round. We found that their major competitor's score had gone from a B+ to an A using the same methodology. The moral is clear: satisfaction is relative to competition; it is not an isolated, trackable measure.

It is important to understand your competitive positions with respect to *satisfaction* and also in terms of *share of wallet*, particularly now in the turbulent economic times where capital budgets are shrinking and the competition is fierce.

There are two basic approaches to gaining this competitive comparison, and they depend on the strategic focus of the vendor. If the focus is primarily on the existing customer base, the first approach will work well. If the strategy is to expand to new customers—both "new to the product" and accounts serviced by competitors—the second approach is more valuable.

The approaches are:

1. **A vendor customer study addressed to the vendor's customer contacts and inquiring both about the experience with the vendor**

as well as one or two competitors. This is a client-identified interview, so the answers regarding the competitor might be biased. In addition, the respondent will be someone selected by the vendor and will possibly be more familiar with the experience with that vendor than with the competitor.

2. **A "blind" study conducted with the relevant roles using a broad universe of potential customers.** Questions are asked about two or more vendors with whom the respondent is familiar. The survey would include both the competitors and the vendor to enable valid comparisons.

In one program, we conduct both approaches. The results were somewhat different between the vendor customer study and the "blind" study, showing higher relative competitor scores in the "blind" study.

Why do customer satisfaction studies fail?

Fred Reichheld of Bain and Company wrote a great book called *The Ultimate Question* that sets out the parameters for the Net Promoter Score approach.

One of the most interesting chapters addressed why some customer satisfaction programs fail.

The key points are set out below:

- Too many surveys, too many questions
- The wrong customers respond.
- Employees don't know how to take corrective action.
- Too many surveys are marketing campaigns in disguise.
- Survey scores don't link to economics.
- Plain vanilla solutions can't meet companies' unique needs.
- There are no generally accepted standards.

- Surveys confuse transactions with relationships.
- Satisfaction studies dissatisfy customers.
- Gaming and manipulation wreck their credibility.

We have experienced specific examples of many of these:

Too many surveys, too many questions

I recently purchased a Ford automobile. The first interesting aspect was that the salesman seemed more interested in receiving the top satisfaction rating from me than even selling me the car.

Having bought the car, I then received a flurry of emails and calls—from the dealership, from the service department in the dealership, from J.D. Power, and from the manufacturer—all with follow-ups and all asking much the same set of questions. I completed the first and ignored the rest. By the time I received the fifth, my satisfaction level with Ford had dropped significantly.

The lesson is clear. If you sell through channels, you should set up a single-survey approach and share the results rather than subject the customer to such an avalanche of communications. It is nearly as bad as being told by an IVR that "your call is important to us" before fighting through a nightmare of choices before being connected to an operator who has been chosen for their low cost rather than their ability and knowledge.

We addressed the frequency aspects above, but the second point—too many questions—is fundamental to a successful program.

What we have seen is that companies believe that they should gather as much information as possible and do not think of the negative impact this can have on the customer.

Again, companies want to be able to track over time, so even as the markets and environments change, they still want to ask the legacy questions. The more dynamic the marketplace is, the more new questions are added until the questionnaire becomes too large and too long to achieve the overall goal of discovering if the customer is satisfied or not, and if not, what is wrong and how it can be rectified.

Some internal factors also contribute to making the survey more difficult for the customer:

- Lots of organizational groups in the vendor are involved (and may be helping fund the program), so they want areas only of interest to them to be included.
- In addition, the organizational structure of the vendor may not appear logical to the customer, who takes a more holistic view of the relationship.
- Lots of different individuals in the vendor organization have attributes that they think are important and want included. These often overlap and are sometimes difficult to communicate if they are too esoteric. Multicollinearity analysis can distill these into a smaller number that will be more understandable and that will make the Customer Experience of completing the survey better.

The wrong customers respond

There are two aspects to this point as well. In market research not everyone takes the survey. In non-customer satisfaction research, the typical completion rate is 1 in 15 of the people invited to take the survey. Market research is based on an assumption that the people responding are random and represent the population.

88

The other aspect is whether the respondent is the right one to represent the customer. As we have said above, there are a lot of different people involved in the buying experience, but then there are others who just use the product. And there are others who are involved in peripheral activities.

In one case, there was a major annoyance in the receiving department because the product was arriving but was not set up for easy offloading. This was not picked up by the regular customer satisfaction program and therefore not addressed. Finally, a salesperson found out about the situation, and it was addressed.

Employees don't know how to take corrective action

Knowing there is a problem and not knowing what to do about it, or—even worse—knowing what to do but not having the resources to address the problem. The cost of the customer satisfaction program is high, and unless it leads to actions that will improve the relationship, it is a waste of money and customer annoyance is increased, as indicated in the following customer response:

They asked me what was wrong and I told them. Then they did nothing. They did not fix the problem and did not communicate with me to tell me they had even considered my (individual) response. They took up my time completing the survey and then ignored it.

In one interesting program, we conducted a pilot and unearthed lots of problem with the relationship. Our client, realistically, realized that there was no near-term fix possible, so they placed the program on hold.

Let's not ask them what the problem is if we have no intention of listening and acting.

It's not the greatest response, but it's more practical than the alternative.

What should your objectives for the CEP measurement be?

CEPs can have a number of objectives:

- Develop a scorecard and use the data.
  - "We scored a B- this year."
- Develop a scorecard and track results over time.
  - *"We scored a B- last year, and this year we got a B."*
- Determine competitive position.
  - *"Although we improved from a B- to a B, our main competitor also improved from a B+ to and A."*
- Isolate problem areas and alert salespeople.
  - *"Fred, did you know that Jeff in ABC Company is really annoyed?"*
- Optimize problem fixes.
  - Concentrate on the "best bang for the buck."
- Improve the relationship with the customer.
  - Connect with the customer and explain why there was a problem and what you are doing about it.
- Improve (profitable) sales to customers.
  - Do not just measure the relationship—improve it.

A full CEP must encompass all of these objectives. If fewer than all seven are implemented, the program can best be described as a customer satisfaction program and that is just fine.

A major objective of the data gathering must be to improve the Customer Experience, not to detract from it. This implies a sensitive approach to the data collection—a short, meaningful questionnaire addressed to the right people and administered professionally. This needs to be followed up by feedback to address specific "complaints" raised in the survey. If you can correct the problems, tell the customer that you have or will. If you cannot correct the issue, explain why and what you can do. There is nothing worse than having a customer spend their time telling you about a problem only to be ignored.

How CE differs from customer satisfaction

Customer satisfaction programs have been undertaken for decades. They primarily address either the customer relationship overall or a sales transaction, the respondent is typically the prime customer contact, and usually there is only one of these surveyed.

CE data collection goes much further and includes:

- All aspects of the customer journey; category awareness, usage over time, etc. are excluded from conventional satisfaction work.
- There is more emphasis on the different roles in the experience.
- There is an emphasis on the touch points.

In addition, CE measurement aims to understand the emotional aspects and not just the factual.

The measurement mechanics are similar for both satisfaction and experience programs, but the measurement is just a small (but critical!) part of the broader CEP, which gains its value from its integration with corporate and product strategy as well as the actions implemented to improve the CE.

CE is a philosophy for corporate management.

Customer Experience Index

We believe that most value comes from the details of the respondents' replies. However, executive management usually wants a single, simple factor that summarizes the full data set. It needs to be easy to understand and easy to explain.

This is often known as a CE Index. Measure this one year and then the next and compare the two. Are we doing better or worse? Also, how does it look overall—good or bad? And how are we doing compared with our competitors?

There have been a number of approaches to this. The simplest is the NPS, an approach developed by Fred Reichheld of Bain and Company and Satmetrix.

The Net Promoter Score, or NPS®, is used to categorize customers into three groups: Promoters, Passives, and Detractors.

The answer to just one question determines into which category a customer fits. The B2B version of the question is typically, "How likely would you be to recommend [vendor] to a colleague or peer?" The Satmetrix version uses a scale of 0–10 where 0 is "totally unlikely" and 10 is "totally likely." The scores are aggregated across a single company with multiple contact points, a country, or some other customer set that the vendor uses. Individual respondents are categorized as:

- Promoters (score 9–10)
- Passives (score 7–8)
- Detractors (score 0–6)

An aggregated NPS score is the percentage of customers in a group who are Promoters less the percentage who are Detractors.

Other approaches use more than the one metric.

In the Office of Citizen Services and Innovative Technologies (OCSIT) at GSA, they have used a four-parameter metric.

- Did your customer accomplish the task that they came to your organization, website, or program for?
- Would your customer recommend your product or service to a friend or colleague? (i.e., NPS)
- Would your customer use your services again?
- How would they rate the overall experience when interacting with your product or service?

In this example, a 1–5 scale is used with the overall score calculated in a similar way to the NPS—the percentage of responses that receive a 4 or 5, minus the responses that rated a 1 or 2.

Forrester Research has used a CE Index based on usefulness, ease of use, and emotional engagement. This score correlates to the NPS but provides understanding of these additional components.

Temkin Group, a Customer Experience consulting firm that specializes in B2C, uses a similar approach.

This approach involves three questions:

Functional experience – Thinking about your recent interactions with us, how effective were we at meeting your needs?

1. Didn't meet any of my needs
2. Met some of my needs
3. Met many of my needs

4. Met most of my needs
5. Met all of my needs

Accessible experience – Thinking about your recent interactions with us, how easy were we to work with?

Not at all easy

1. Slightly easy
2. Moderately easy
3. Very easy
4. Extremely easy

Emotional experience – Thinking about your recent interactions with us, how enjoyable were the interactions?

1. Not at all enjoyable
2. Slightly enjoyable
3. Moderately enjoyable
4. Very enjoyable
5. Extremely enjoyable

Another approach is to include retention and up-sell/cross-sell as two additional indexes to support the NPS. These three indexes are the parameters used by ForSee in its offerings. These additional indexes may or may not be applicable to each vendor.

One client uses a combination of three measures:

• Overall satisfaction
• Willingness to continue buying
• Willingness to recommend

Their overall score is an average of scores on these three.

Defining the CE metric

The raw scores will come back from the research program as a set of 0–10 scores, or in some cases, 1–7 or 1–5 or whatever.

The raw scores can be used, but it is better to normalize these to a 0–100 scale. Thus a "7.8" on a 0–10 scale becomes "78."

The objectives of the CEP need to drive the metrics

The CEP team needs to develop target metrics for the company. These will depend on a number of aspects and relate to where the vendor is today in its Customer Experience rating, the role of competition, etc.

Our targets should include actually gaining a particular rating (e.g., overall 80 or higher). They should also include a measure of gap over our competitors and a year-on-year improvement. The targets, as with all targets, should reflect the reality—if we are actually poor at Customer Experience, let's set attainable targets with improvement targets over a number of years.

Typically, we shall want to display the results in a scorecard or a dashboard with several aspects shown. The following sets out an example:

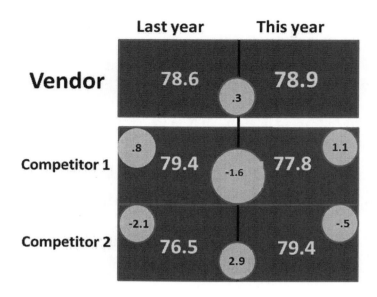

	Last year	This year
Vendor	78.6	78.9
		.3
Competitor 1	.8 79.4	77.8 1.1
	-1.6	
Competitor 2	-2.1 76.5	79.4 -.5
	2.9	

In the example, we have an overall CE index of 78.9 this year, which compares favorably with last year's score—an improvement of .3. Last year we were behind Competitor 1, but they have fallen back, and we now have a 1.1 point lead. Regarding Competitor 2, we had a strong lead over them last year (2.1 points), but they improved dramatically (by 2.9 points) are now beating us by .5 points.

Each element can be color coded to reflect a level of performance compared with the target.

For each segment being measured, we would present this matrix for both the global and the segment results.

Different dashboard designs appeal to different people and/or companies. Some like them with little information and shown graphically; others like tables of data. More on this later.

Transition from customer satisfaction to CE - the CEP organization and team

Customer satisfaction is sometimes managed at a relatively low level in a vendor organization. The staffing can be quite junior, and their skill set can relate more to market research than to steering the company's culture and strategy.

The shift to CE may require a higher-level team with skills in a number of areas:

- "Consulting" on the strategy aspects of a CEP—the ability to work with senior management, including the CEO; explaining the processes; selling the concept and then having a "seat at the table" during implementation and beyond; specifically, political awareness, persuasion, understanding the insights, managing workshops and presentations, working with business management to develop options for actions to tackle problems, introducing the CE strategy question into strategy-planning sessions
- Organizational skills, including the ability to develop and "sell" the framework aspects
- Ability to work with people at all levels to present results and drive action but also to address the essential details (e.g., collect valid sample record data)
- Sound market research skills—questionnaire development, sampling strategy, analysis plan, advanced analytical skills
- Administrative skills—assembling the customer contact sample data, cleaning it, handling duplicates/errors, handling pre-notification

In the full CEP context, the head of the CEP should report to the CEO, perhaps though the COO. Even if the CEP reports farther down in the organization, for it to be successful, it should have a clear access to the CEO since it is he/she who will be applying CE to the culture and strategy of the company overall.

If the CE scores are used to set and measure executive performance, it is fundamental that this group is independent of those executives who are being measured by the scores.

Use of the customer satisfaction/experience score to remunerate executives

It is quite common for the scores from customer satisfaction studies to be used as part of a formula for rewarding individuals in the vendor organization.

There are pluses and minuses with this approach.

On the positive side, individuals take the program seriously and should be striving to improve the Customer Experience. This can be anyone from the sales representative up to the CEO.

But be careful of the formula. Sometimes a sales representative will be dinged for poor customer satisfaction when the customer is just annoyed by the product quality, which is not the representative's fault nor within his/her control.

In addition, with money on the line, a sales representative with an unhappy customer is likely to find a reason that the customer should not be surveyed—"We are just starting a tricky new sales negotiation." He may also emulate my Ford dealer salesman who spent a huge amount of effort to convince me to rate him as "Excellent" on everything—not a good endorsement for the vendor.

Linkage with remuneration will also result in the survey results being questioned. In one case, the customer had given a low satisfaction score, and the sales representative was convinced that he did not really mean this, so he challenged the results. The vendor team insisted that we change the results to reflect what the sales representative thought. He may have been right or not, but we refused to change the data and subsequently resigned that account.

14: MEASUREMENT - THE MECHANICS

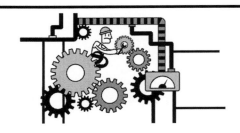

Garbage in, garbage out

The term "garbage in, garbage out" was first used in 1963 in a newspaper article about the early stages of computerization of the United States Internal Revenue Service. It still applies today.

If the fundamental data being collected for measurement of the Customer Experience Program is flawed, the result and the actions following this will also be flawed.

Unfortunately, there is a naïve belief that providing data that passes a "smell test" is as good as data gathered in a much more rigorous manner. Unlike the prerecession days, corporations are fixated on lowering costs and often close their eyes to poor data collection that an internal purchasing group has managed to acquire at the lowest cost.

I needed a brain tumor removed, so I chose the specialist who would do it for 15% less than the others.

Not a good idea!

Collecting the data

While Customer Experience is a philosophy of corporate management, the measurement of this and the identification of what is wrong comes from listening to the customer—and usually, listening to the customers' answers to specific questions. This requires data collection, and the market research industry has been fuelled by this over many decades.

There are some basic questions that need to be addressed when establishing the measurement aspects of the CEP. These are similar to customer satisfaction programs, but with the increased value expected from a CEP, the answers might be different.

The first aspects relate to the overall study:

Client-identified vs. blind

Most CEPs use a "client-identified" approach. The vendor provides a list of their customers—with contact details—to the agency conducting the interviews, and that agency states clearly, up front, to the respondents the name of the vendor sponsoring the study. Providing the customer approves this, the results of each interview with the name of the respondent can then be passed back to the vendor for action.

The alternative is when the vendor does not supply a list of customers, and the research agency uses its own lists, screening for the vendor's customers. On occasion, the vendor may supply a list of customers but without the contact details. In these cases, the study is conducted "blind," and the vendor is not identified to the respondent. Also, market research association rules prohibit the agency from revealing the identity of the respondent.

There are a number of characteristics of each approach:

Client-identified

Pros:

- Sound ability to respond directly to issues at a customer level
- Linkage to vendor's customer databases
- Higher response rates

Cons:

- Possibility of biased response—both for the vendor and competitors
- Sometimes higher cost owing to efforts on vendor side to acquire and manage sample, fatiguing, and satisfying "do not survey" requirements
- Potentially political issues

Blind

Pros:

- Lower cost
- No political issues
- No biased response

Cons:

- Only generic feedback to customers
- No tie-in to vendor's customer databases
- No ability to resolve individual issues

Specific difficulties with a client-identified program include:

- Country-level or business-unit push back – "We shall do it ourselves in our country. My cousin has a research firm that will be unbiased."
- Sales-representative level – "Not with my accounts, you don't. We have a major contract being negotiated—you cannot interfere. No, I have not registered the opportunity yet."
- Identification of potential respondents by sales people will often lead to the "promoters" being selected.
- If satisfaction levels are linked to remuneration, there are significant areas of conflict.

Achieving comparable data for competitor assessments is problematic.

We recommend a hybrid approach with a client-identified customer study coupled with a broader, blind study to address both the vendor and the competitors in a robust way.

Formal or informal?

In customer satisfaction, if you have relatively few customers, you can use an informal approach. A senior manager or executive can call each of the main contacts every quarter and ask, "How are things going?"

There will be a host of different areas discussed, and each customer can be addressed independently. The feedback regarding a customer's problems and how these can be addressed can be covered in subsequent calls. It is important that the executive making the call is not in sales and does not have any vested interest in a good or bad score.

This approach can also be used with Tier 1 customers in companies with a lot of customers but a manageable group comprising the highest tier.

For Tier 2, Tier 3, etc., a more formal approach is needed—a questionnaire administered uniformly and analysis undertaken. If you go down this route, it is probably a good idea to administer the same questionnaire with the Tier 1 customers to see if the problems are the same or different.

In-house or external agency

With the number of self-service questionnaire tools available today, there is a cost saving that can be had by administering a CEP in-house. For small companies with, say, fewer than 200 customers, this may be fine, but there can still be errors made in constructing the questionnaire, getting the sample right, analyzing the data, and drawing insights that will lead to action.

If you want to make this look professional, you should have a qualified market research firm develop and test the questionnaire, even if you administer the survey yourself.

As you move into a full CEP, the measurement becomes more than a scorecard and requires the rigor that you can usually get only from a professionally managed approach. In addition, the aim must be to use the survey as a way of saying to the customer, "We care, we want to know, and we shall act."

Using an outside firm adds to that credibility, and some customers will be guarded unless they are assured of the confidentiality an external, independent agency can provide.

An external agency can make this happen. This agency will provide to your management a third-party endorsement of the results, and their expertise will affect the response rate and the quality of the result. For example, a research agency will know when to send out email invitations to a web survey, and they will know how to word the invitation to avoid spam filters.

Quantitative or qualitative

A quantitative survey allows robust aggregation of results. Ask 500 customers exactly the same question, and you can rely on the results to be representative of the population (of, say, 10,000).

In addition, with 500 respondents, you can probably analyze the data across various dimensions—by product group, by geography, by customer tier.

Qualitative is best used at either the development stage of the quantitative questionnaire (What do I want to ask about?), or after the quantitative to go back to specific customers whose answers were "interesting." Normally the qualitative follow-up hones in on customers who are not happy (who are manifested in low NPS scores or simply low scores in overall satisfaction or loyalty).

These interviews should be conducted by an independent third party, but this must be someone who can talk in a "peer-to-peer" relationship with the customer.

The in-depth interviews should be no more than half an hour and can be recorded (providing the customer agrees to this). This is a great opportunity to have a freewheeling discussion, including what the customer thinks the vendor should do to remedy any deficiencies. Asking how competitors avoid these problems gives additional insight.

Web vs. telephone quantitative interviews

Historically B2B quantitative interviews have been conducted by telephone, and this is still the case for many programs, particularly if an objective of the program is to show your customers that you are professional and that you care.

Recently, many programs have either switched completely to a web survey or at least offer this as an alternative to the telephone survey. The web survey is significantly less expensive to administer and allows the respondent to complete it at their own pace and in their own time. Open-ended comments are sometimes recorded more accurately when the respondent types them in; in telephone interviews, the interviewer needs to key these in either during the interview or from a recording afterwards.

Response rates for telephone surveys are usually better, and the interviewer can probe for answers better than in a web survey. In addition, call recording allows the vendor's management to listen directly to the "voice of the customer."

Each case is different, but assuming you have accurate email addresses, we would recommend a hybrid approach with email invitations to a web survey being sent out first, and then, if there is no reply, a telephone interview should be attempted.

Comparability of web and telephone responses

Web and telephone interviews use somewhat different methodologies. In web interviews, the respondent works at his/her own pace without prompts from an interviewer. They can deal with longer lists of alternative responses that they can see, whereas in a telephone interview, there is no visual stimulus. The questionnaires can be worded somewhat differently as well; the web interview can be terser, whereas the telephone interview is more conversational.

The question is whether the results are sufficiently different, requiring some adjustment be made to the data. And if there is a difference, which is the more correct?

From the large number of studies we have undertaken using mixed methodology, we have found some differences seemingly caused by people being likely to be more critical in writing than on the phone when talking with an interviewer.

Overall, the differences are small and probably not worth an attempt to make any adjustment.

Aspects related to web surveys

Email invitations and reminders

For web-based interviews, an email is sent to all customer contacts inviting them to take the survey. Typically the customer clicks on an embedded link and is transferred to a website where the questionnaire is administered.

The email invitation is critical to the completion rate of the study. Everyone receives hundreds of emails each day, and many are filtered out as spam. Even if the spam filter does not discard the invitation, customers will themselves delete scores of emails if they appear to be uninteresting, such as invitations to webinars, offers of discounts, and other marketing material. If your email invitation has an unknown "sender" or a subject line that does not resonate, the likelihood is that the email will not even be opened. One of the values that a research firm brings is advice on what the current rules (they change all the time) for the spam filter engines are and how best to phrase both the subject line and the body text of the email. Beyond that there are phrases that are attractive in the subject line and those that are not.

For the subject line in a CEP, we most often use something like "[Vendor name] Customer Experience Program," and the sender is set out as the research agency name. This presupposes that a prenotification has already been sent out. See below.

When to send emails for best response

When we arrive at work in the morning, there is always a stack of emails, and the first thing we do is delete most of them. Later in the day, we are getting a trickle and can devote a little more time to deciding what to delete and what to read. Studies have shown that Monday or Tuesday (it used to be Tuesday, but now this is the peak day for email!) is the best day to send email to optimize the customer's attention. And this is further optimized either between 9 and 10 a.m. or between 3 and 4 p.m. The worst response can be assumed if the email is delivered over the weekend.

Remember—these days and times are when you want the email delivered. If you are sending email invitations to China from the United Kingdom, for example, with the time change you need these to be sent at 1:30 p.m. on Sunday—the equivalent of 9:30 a.m. Monday in China.

When do you send the reminders?

After the initial invitation, some customers will respond and others will not. After a period of three to four days or even one week, a reminder should be sent to those who have not responded. After another three to four days, a second reminder can be sent but no more. For Tier 1 customers, a telephone follow-up is generally more effective than the second reminder.

Hybrid web/phone methodology

While web interviews are less costly, phone interviews usually achieve higher response rates and certainly show the customer that we think he/

she is important. Sometimes, customers prefer a web interview that they can complete at their leisure, perhaps in several "sittings." Others prefer the telephone interview.

In the hybrid study, we send email invitations first but also allow the customer to say that they would prefer a telephone interview. Typically, we have used an appointment scheduler that is built in to the beginning of the web questionnaire so that the customer can set a day and time for the telephone interview. The telephone interviewer calls at that time and completes the interview.

For Tier 1 customers, it is appropriate to provide this option, but for lower tiers, the phone option may not even be offered.

In some cases, we may wish to have the telephone interviewer simply encourage the response to compete the web survey. In this case, the interviewer and the supporting software should allow the interviewer to send a new link in real time in case the respondent has lost or deleted the email invitation. An even better approach is if the interviewer can provide a short URL to access the survey and then provide a code that will link the interview with the sample file. In cases where the respondent agrees to start the interview immediately, the interviewer should be able to monitor the initial responses and stay with the respondent until the interview has been started. This can significantly reduce the attrition rate of interview completion.

Aspects related to telephone surveys

International programs

Most B2B Customer Experience Programs are in companies where the customer base is international. This adds an extra challenge for "getting it right." There are language issues as well as cultural issues. And if you are using a telephone methodology, you need international interviewers who can deliver a consistent result—web is much easier.

In terms of language, some vendors assert that their customer base speaks English anyway, and so they want to conduct the survey in English only. This does not save a huge amount of cost and really is an insult to your customers:

> *They wanted me to spend my time completing the survey and did not have the courtesy to use my own language. Why should I respond?*

The normal approach is to develop the questionnaire in the company's own language—English for the United States, German for German companies, etc., and when tested and approved have it translated into the other languages relating to countries to be studied. A second stage is "back translation" where the foreign-language version is translated back into English by another translator with the expectation that the new English version will match the original.

This approach will be similar for both telephone and web methodologies, but it is important that the translation is undertaken and back-translated by people who know the interview process and who translate in a colloquial way rather than a formal approach as used in written prose, agreements, etc.

There will always be criticisms about the translations. Any two highly competent translators will phrase things differently and might have serious arguments. We have found that this is particularly the case in German. The back-translation is useful to cross-check the accuracy. Often the vendor's in-country staff insists on checking the translations that are to be used with their customers. This can lead to rounds of discussions and arguments and can result in a compromised questionnaire. The saying that "a camel is actually a horse designed by a committee" is appropriate.

Also, sometimes country management would like a different set of questions or wording. They will alter the translation to provide this, and this will result in answers to a different question, which makes aggregation and comparison flawed.

Verbatim or open-ended question responses may also need to be translated and/or transcribed. More on this later.

Assuming the translations are accurate, the question remains whether there are any differences in responses that can be expected owing to cultural differences. In studies that we have conducted, there are minor differences, but usually these contribute only about one point difference—and that was based on large B2C markets. Our recommendation has been not to make any adjustment and have to explain the biases for this. With the rapid globalization, these minor differences are reducing every day.

Central control

In the early days of RONIN (in 1986), we were asked by a global B2B company to bid on a customer satisfaction study across some 20 countries. In those days, we did not have a research group—we were marketing consultants—but we did know the global scene well and had good ties to the potential client.

We decided to bid on the job and attempted to find a market research firm to partner with. We wanted to find one that could field the program across those 20 countries. And in those pre-Internet days, telephone interviewing was the preferred approach.

We approached many of the big players, but all said they would handle their home country and provide us a list of either subsidiaries or partners in the other countries and we should cut separate deals with each—not what we had in mind.

We made some phone calls to these companies but did not find them very responsive. Each had its own approach. Some used computer-assisted telephone interviewing (CATI) systems, some used pencil and paper, and some insisted that a face-to-face interview was the only viable approach. The CATI systems were not uniform.

This was not going to work.

We found a few agencies that covered more than one country, but finally resolved the issue in 1995 when we established our own data collection telephone interviewing center in London, England. London is the only place in the world that met our criteria: all nationalities available for interviewing in their native language, English as a second language (for briefing and management), and people with a high skill level who would work in a call-center environment (mainly students doing pre- or postgraduate work at colleges in London).

This centralized model allows for consistent briefing and management, use of one, standard questionnaire, and flexibility to make necessary changes rapidly and seamlessly. Overall quality control is a given.

This model has become more standard over the years, but still many international studies are split up over a number of diverse, in-country agencies.

In the past decade, the central model has become more prevalent. Web-based interviewing is logically undertaken from one central system, and software used for telephone interviewing has evolved to be web-based so that interviewers in China access the questionnaire over the Internet through a browser; the managing agency (perhaps in the United States) can then monitor what is being asked and make corrections to understanding etc. from a remote location.

Call recording and the portal

It is common to record all telephone interviews in CE research. No matter how good the interviewers are and the background administration is, certain customers will complain to their sale representatives. Also, if a customer is particularly upset, the vendor will want to listen to the dialog directly.

If each telephone interview (including open-ended questions) is recorded, a portal can be set up to enable easy access for vendor staff and management to listen to these interviews.

Typically, the vendor will review closed-end results and then access the recording of specific respondents.

Bear in mind that the interviews (and recordings) will be in the local language.

> In one engagement, a senior executive from our client had a set of interviews downloaded to his iPhone so that he could listen to them on the plane trip to China. These were Chinese interviews, and he quickly discovered that these were in Chinese, a language he did not speak.

Obviously, the interviewer needs to clear with the customer that the interview will be recorded and needs to get the respondent's permission for this. It is important that the recordings are managed properly and are available only to responsible members of the vendor team.

Dealing with Voice mail

When undertaking telephone interviews, the interviewer calls in to the respondent's telephone number (perhaps through a switchboard) and attempts to connect with the respondent. The pre-notification is useful as is the appointment scheduler, but too often the interviewer reaches the respondent's voice mail.

What to do?

This situation should have been anticipated, and the interviewer should leave a scripted message encouraging the respondent to call back to a toll-free number to take the interview. In some cases, we have had the interviewer also trigger (through software) an email that has a link to an appointment scheduler.

In previous days, when voice mail was not as prevalent, if the respondent did not answer, the interviewer would hang up and call back later. These days, voice mail is used by the respondent as a screening mechanism.

Appointment scheduler

This is a web-based portal for use, globally, by the sales force to schedule appointments for their customers.

The sales representative visits the customer, tells them about the survey, and schedules a call from an interviewer for a particular time and particular day. Other details—telephone number, etc.—are verified with the respondent, and at the appointed time, the interviewer calls and conducts the interview.

This sounds fairly trivial, but it results in completion rates of about 15% higher than had been experienced prior to the process being set up.

The questionnaire

There is no physical limit to the length of a questionnaire, but particularly when you want to improve and not decrease a positive Customer Experience, the shorter the better. The NPS approach says the answer to just one question is sufficient, but exploring a number of attributes is invariably required to understand the areas where the vendor is doing well and those where there is room for improvement.

Overall, the interview should be kept to six to nine minutes. Interestingly, we implemented an *ad hoc* transaction study recently where there was only one question—How did the maintenance call go? If the respondent answered, "Just fine," that was it. If he said "terrible," we followed up with a request to tell us what was wrong. This in turn was followed by, "What would you expect the vendor to do to ensure this is not a problem the future?" Another question was, "Have you had these problems with other vendors?" The answers to these questions are all open ended; they are not the normal survey questions that ask for an answer in terms of a set of pre-coded responses.

Dealing with open-ended responses

Most CEP questionnaires use primarily "closed-end" questions. These ask a question and provide a multiple choice set of responses, which allows easy tabulation of results and consistent data for use in advanced analytical models. The results of the data can be presented in a variety of forms: arithmetic means ("We achieved an average of 6.2 on a 1-7 scale"), as a median ("Most customers rate us as a 6 on a 1-7 scale"), or as a top-box metric ("74% of customers rated us as 'top box'—either 6 or 7"). Each approach has its value; the key is to present trending data consistently.

When a set of attributes are predefined, it is possible (perhaps likely) that they will not cover what the real problem is. Particularly as we move to Customer Experience, we have a much more emotion-based view from the customer, not just "Was it delivered on time? – Yes/No."

The alternative is to ask "open-ended" questions that solicit a nonstructured reply. "What could our client do to improve the experience?"

In CE, we need to be asking a more emotional set of questions, and individuals will respond with emotional answers:

> *I just did not like the sales representative. He was good but there was just something about him ….*

> *Most people do not care about how good the website is. But I find it terrible that a professional company cannot do better.*

Open-ended answers are more difficult to collect using traditional multiple-choice questioning approaches. Asking the question is easy, but the answers are more problematic. If a web survey is used, the customer needs to key in his/her answer and may be reticent to commit this to writing. A telephone interviewer can achieve a better response but needs to be able to record this successfully.

One of the best approaches is for one or more people in the vendor organization to either listen to the recordings (if telephone) or read the actual written answers (web). Telephone interviews are typically recorded and translated, and transcripts can be prepared, albeit at a cost.

The main difficulty is in analysis. With this open-ended approach, there will be a wider range in responses than normal. As such, coding the responses will often end up with a large number of categories, which will be difficult to convert to actions.

Coding

The traditional approach to analyzing open-ended responses has been to develop a code frame first. This comprises a set of response categories into which we expect the open ends to fit. For example, we might expect the issues raised in the open end to relate to:

- Cost
- Delivery
- Product, etc.

The code frame may be kept static over time or may be constructed each time from manual analysis of, say, the first hundred interviews. This can be modified later. Then, a member of the coding staff reviews each open end manually and allocates it to one or more coding categories.

"Our last order was late and did not work when installed" would be categorized as both "delivery" and "product," perhaps with subcategories. Analysis is then undertaken on the codes: "28% of customers find fault with our delivery process."

In telephone interviews, the interviewer can write down or key in the open-ended responses, but this can be slow and inaccurate. When the call center has call recording, the open ends can be accessed at a later time and transcribed.

For web-based interviews, the open ends are entered directly by the respondent.

The processing of the open ends will depend on how they will be used. Processing options include:

- Translation into English
- Transcription in local language

- Transcription in English
- Coding and analysis

In one scenario, country management will be the only users and will want to review all the comments. Transcription in the local language is all that is needed.

In another case, we may be interested only in the analysis of the coded responses. The coding can be undertaken within the foreign language, and neither translation nor transcriptions is required.

It is important to determine the likely use so that expense and time is not incurred when it is unnecessary.

> In one case, the vendor insisted that all recordings be translated and transcribed daily; this presented a huge cost and administrative nightmare. Few of the transcripts were even used.

Manual coding is a time-consuming and costly exercise. For web-based interviews, when the respondent provides a written answer, analysis can be attempted using automated text-analysis software. This has become popular in analyzing huge quantities of text, typically in blogs and social media sites, and is used in a B2C environment. The software is currently similar in maturity to automatic language translation software; it is an inexpensive approach, but often the results are poor. It will no doubt evolve in the future, but today there are many difficulties and errors.

In the B2B context, the data collected is less and the subjects more complex. We believe for the present that the "old-fashioned" approach of manual coding, while costly, delivers a much more accurate result.

Before we leave this section, let me stress the value of just reading or listening to the open-ended responses. An executive can acquire a much better understanding of the emotional aspects of the customer from these open ends. In our sales representative notification approach, open ends, in both English and the local language, are seen as one of the most valuable deliverables.

However, there is still a need (and cost) to "clean" these. In web interviews particularly, the respondent will not necessarily care about grammar and spelling and may use "texting-like" abbreviations. Before these are passed to the vendor team, they need to be "cleaned."

Should we keep the survey the same – changing horses in midstream?

There is always a debate about keeping the questions the same over time (to allow valid comparison of the results) or changing them.

"We can change questions whenever you like."

"Why would we want to do that?"

"The marketplace is dynamic, as is your strategy."

"We have been using the same questions for over 10 years. They work."

"Really?"

One use of a CEP is to track changes in the customer base over time. Keeping the same questions allows that, but a slavish use of out-of-date questions does not serve the business well. The NPS question(s) might remain the same, but many of the others will logically change.

Change can also come from changes in customer sets (to match new organization structure), touch points, and roles. Changes are always possible, but additional effort is always required to match the new with the old without false comparisons being made.

It may seem trivial, but the timing for the change and its impact on reporting, dashboards, etc. is important at an operational level.

Privacy/data protection, etc.

Data collected from customers (and prospects) needs to be treated carefully. The research agency will know all the rules and adhere to them.

In addition, there is legislation enacted in many countries about privacy that needs to be followed. The agreements between the United States and the European Union regarding transportation of data at an individual level (as opposed to in aggregate or when no identification of individual responses to an individual is contained) are embodied in the Safe Harbor agreement. Most vendors will have signed up for this anyway to allow CRM systems to function internationally, but it is worth checking. The easiest way is to go to https://safeharbor.export.gov/list.aspx where you can check to see if your company and your research agency are registered and current.

There is a high likelihood, following the recent NSA issues, that more countries will prohibit data at an individual level from being stored outside the country of origin. This has not been aimed at B2B research programs but may be so broad as to encompass this.

The CEP team should keep a vigilant eye on this, coordinating through the vendor's privacy executive.

Sample

In order to conduct interviews, we need to have a list of the customers we would like to interview and contact details (email address for web, telephone number for telephone). In CEPs, these are typically your customers, so it seems that it would be easy to get this sample information.

In fact, even in the largest and most sophisticated vendors, this is not the case. Usually this data is held in a CRM system used by the sales force to manage their accounts. As we have said before, salespeople are paid to sell, not to do administration; because of this, the CRM system is often out of date or incomplete. The salesperson will often restrict access to individuals who will likely provide a bad score. A rigorous customer database will make this easier, but still the data is unlikely to be 100% correct. And in some cases, there are multiple sources of samples, with each in its own format. Management of the sample can be a major nightmare.

In addition, obviously, if we omit individuals who are likely to give a bad score, we shall end up with an erroneous result.

The sample will usually be the vendor's first-level contact. And that person will not reflect the variety of roles in the customer and will have a "point of sale" view, rather than addressing the entire customer journey. Touch points important to other roles may not be important to this individual.

Sample management by the research agency can be complex if the sample is delivered piecemeal, in different formats, with duplicates and of poor quality. This results in potential errors, a delay while the sample is checked and formatted, and increased cost.

As discussed previously, it is important not to over-survey your customers.

Most vendors have a two-stage approach to prevent an individual from being approached when this is not appropriate. The first stage is "do not survey"—if the individual has stated that they do not wish to undertake surveys. Normally, a flag on the customer record identifies these people. This "do not survey" flag may be implemented across all individuals in the customer company if there is a blanket policy that prohibits individuals from undertaking surveys.

The second stage is a "fatigue" flag that prevents individuals from being harassed by too many surveys. A metric for "fatigue" needs to be determined (e.g., do not attempt to survey more than once every two months) and then used.

How frequently should you test satisfaction and experience?

The frequency of measuring customer satisfaction and CE depends on a number of items. The first is the type of study—transactional or relationship. For expediency, you may wish to conduct the relationship study on a continuous basis, but you should only survey any one customer on an annual basis. More frequently will create a less satisfied customer!

An exception to this is to go back to customers who have shown dissatisfaction and retest this after improvements have been made in their areas of dissatisfaction. For example, if a customer is displeased with the ease of use of the vendor website, it would make sense to go back after improvements are made to test that the problem has been corrected and to display to the customer that "we have listened and made changes."

Transactional studies can be undertaken more frequently but should be limited to no more than three to four times each year. Transactional studies should be undertaken as a continuous program to allow early detection of any systemic problems and to allow these to be addressed quickly.

The total CE score and driver attributes

We discussed the use of a CE Index, which aims to encapsulate all the measured variables into one index. Executive management love this since it is simple to understand and can provide a comparison between the CE Index of competitors and over time.

> "See we are better than Competitors A and B."

> "Hey, we have improved over last year."

And a composite:

> "We are better than last year, but Competitor C improved more."

Management then wants to be able to "drill down," particularly when they want to fix things that are problems.

The first pass at this relates to "where" the problem is. Is it across all geographic regions? Is it in one business unit? This analysis can come from "slicing and dicing" using a model or a dashboard.

The next level relates to what "drives" the score, and it's called (you will never guess) driver analysis. By constructing a set of attributes that are expected to be drivers of the score (e.g., an understanding of the customer's business), the impact of a high or low score on this attribute on the total CE score gives insight into what is or is not important. For example, if a high score on "understanding the customer's business" is seen to drive a high CE score, then making sure that understanding the customer's business is a high priority.

The development of the list of attributes to be tested is key to the CEP. The list cannot be too long, or we shall upset the customer. The maximum we recommend is ten although fewer are better.

One approach is to have a set that covers the main aspects of the relationship and touch points and then to have "drill downs" on some where the customer provides a low score. Thus, if a customer rates the "interaction with the sales team" low, a follow-up question(s) will seek to achieve a deeper understanding of the issue.

Often the attributes, particularly if there are many of these, will end up measuring (almost) the same aspect. This is called multicollinearity, and statistical techniques can be used to determine where this is the case. If two attributes measure the same aspect, drop one of them. Why burden the customer with unnecessary questions?

Incentives

When using web surveys, an incentive of some kind is generally offered. This can comprise a cash payment, a sweepstake prize, a copy of research findings, or a gift voucher. In B2B interviews, the incentive is typically required and is of much higher value than in consumer surveys where often there is no incentive at all. If you are using a panel that purports to be a B2B panel but the incentive is low or there is no incentive, beware—this is probably a consumer panel.

In telephone surveys an incentive is rarely offered.

For customer satisfaction or CE programs, an incentive is not used; however, if the questionnaire is long and complicated and/or if a number of other topics are covered, an incentive may be appropriate. And if you use a "blind" study, an incentive is appropriate.

Interview alerts to salespeople (and their management)

One major value of a CEP is the rapid feedback of customer opinions regardless of whether they are good or bad.

If the comments are bad, the sales representative can follow up with the customer quickly to rectify the problem. At a more aggregated level, systemic issues can be discovered early and rectified. If the comments are good, this is a great motivator for the sales representative to see what their customer has said and to accept the accolade.

Details should include the full interview with the customer's responses to each question. Verbatim answers should be shown in the local language and also translated.

Interview alerts should be generated directly from either the web survey or the computer-assisted telephone interviewing software and emailed either directly to the sales representative (and manager) or through an intermediary. In many cases, these are sent only if the responses from the customer meet some low threshold (e.g., overall satisfaction is less than 8 on a 0-10 scale). The questionnaire software can easily manage this.

> The rapidity of emailing needs to be adjusted to the customer situation. We set up a system for an online brokerage firm, and the system fired off an email in real time as soon as the first negative threshold was breeched. In one case, early in the program, a customer was still working on the interview when a service representative called to try to rectify the problem. The speed of the response was startling and conjured up

a "big brother" image. We built a half-hour delay into the system from when the interview had been fully completed.

Pre-notification

In CE, as with all research, the emphasis is to complete as many interviews as possible. Pre-notification can help here.

In pre-notification, the vendor sends a communication alerting the customer that they will shortly be contacted by the independent research agency that is authorized to undertake the interview.

The method of doing this varies. In the IT industry, email is ubiquitous; regular mail is unnecessary and probably has a negative impact. In farm machinery, a regular letter has more impact.

The communication should set out the objectives of the study, the time scale, and an identification that the research agency is legitimate and authorized to do the work for the vendor. It should be signed by a senior executive in the vendor organization, preferably one that the customer knows or knows of. For a CEP, a notification from the CEO is appropriate.

Although email can be "aliased" so that it appears to be coming from the CEO but is actually coming from the research agency, this can be uncovered easily by anyone with technical knowledge and should be avoided. The logistics of getting the emails out from the CEO's office to coincide with the survey rollout can be difficult and should be planned well in advance. If the study is continuous, it is somewhat easier if it is a regular weekly event.

Obviously, pre-notifications must be in the local language and use local conventions for salutations, etc. This sounds easy, but there are some major pitfalls.

In-depth follow-up

The quantitative interview tends to be a set of multiple-choice questions allowing easy and consistent aggregation of results. Even open-ended responses can be brief and not get to the nub of the issue.

We have found that there can be huge value from conducting follow-up, in-depth interviews. This needs to be conducted by an outside agency, and the interviewer should be able talk with the customer on a peer-to-peer basis. Customers can vent if they want to, but most are constructive in describing what their peeves are, how competitors may be dealing with them, and what they expect from the vendor.

Getting the data set right before analysis – the magic numbers

When undertaking analysis, you would expect that a set of 500 completed interviews would be five times more accurate than a set of 100. In fact, statistically the 500 set is much better, but not five times better. Statistically, the higher the sample size the better, but often neither the practicality nor the budget will allow you to reach a high number.

Practically, in market research, some "magic numbers" have become the minimum acceptable numbers for analysis:

- At least 50 minimum for summary statistics (e.g., mean or "top box") or correlational analysis
- At least 10 responses per variable when using advanced analytical techniques (e.g., driver analysis, Structured Equation Modeling [SEM]). So for an SEM with 20 variables, we would require 200 respondents. A minimum of 100 in total is needed, even if only a few variables are being analyzed.

The actual numbers rely on a host of factors, including how many variables you have and how correlated the items are. If you only need a scorecard of performance rather than the more useful aspects of a CEP, keep your data to a minimum. Why pay more than you need to?

However, bear in mind that you need these volumes (50 or 100) for each cell of data that you wish to analyze. Thus, if you want to analyze at a country level and you operate in 20 countries, you will need 50 in each of those 20 countries—1,000 in total.

How to lie with statistics – weighting of data

How to Lie with Statistics is a book written by Darrell Huff in 1954 presenting an introduction to statistics for the general reader. He explains how factual data can be represented in such a way that it tells whatever story is required. A chart comparing several years of data but starting after a particularly good or bad year shows a different story. Saying a stock gained 10% today does not draw attention to the fact that it lost 12% yesterday. Even a chart that shows volatility but whose base is set at yesterday's closing and shows changes against that can distort the "fact" that the increase of 150 points on a base of 15,000 is hardly worth mentioning.

The CEP team may then need to explain to management that when data is aggregated, it may need to be adjusted. Oh, oh, sounds fishy!

As set out above, if you can collect a totally random set of responses that are representative of the marketplace, there is not a problem. Probability theory takes care of the problem. A CE mean of 6.8 means just that—6.8.

So if we want to be able to report on each of the, say, 20 countries in which a company operates, you will need to collect 50 interviews in each country—a total of 1,000. Analysis on a country level is just fine, but there is a potential for trouble if you just take the arithmetic mean of all 1,000 since not every country is equal. A low score in a few very small countries can have a significant impact on the overall score.

The approach we have to take is to "weight" the data to correct for lack of a representative sample.

Take the example below:

	Sample	Country Mean	GDP	Weight based on GDP
US	50	6.3	15.7	0.30
Japan	50	5.4	6	0.11
China	50	5.6	8.2	0.15
Korea	50	7.1	1.2	0.02
Germany	50	6.3	3.4	0.06
France	50	6.7	2.6	0.05
UK	50	6.5	2.4	0.05
Italy	50	6.9	2	0.04
Spain	50	6.2	1.4	0.03
Brazil	50	4.1	2.4	0.05
Argentina	50	4.2	0.5	0.01
Singapore	50	6.3	0.3	0.01
Malaysia	50	6.2	0.3	0.01
Canada	50	4.2	1.8	0.03
Australia	50	5.6	1.5	0.03
Greece	50	2.1	0.3	0.01
Thailand	50	2.3	0.4	0.01
South Africa	50	3.5	0.4	0.01
Russia	50	2.1	2	0.04
Portugal	50	2.1	0.2	0.00
GLOBAL		5.0		5.7

The correct rating for, say, Argentina, is 4.2 from column 3, but the global, overall average (5.0) is skewed and should be weighted to make the composite data more representative. In this case we have used the GDP of each country to reflect the weight. The sum of the final column—5.7—is a more accurate reflection than the unweighted 5.0.

In this example, we have used a weight based on 2012 GDP, but actual weights need to be selected based on the product set (e.g., for computer hardware the estimated IT spend for each country is a better measure; for tractors, the square acreage of farmland may be appropriate).

Weighting has its drawbacks:

- It can be difficult to explain to nonmarket research management.
- Management will suspect manipulation.
- If results do not match what management want, they will likely question the weighting.
- It can become a mechanism for "getting to the right answer."
- Deciding on the optimal weighting approach can be tricky.

If you have to weight:

- Make it simple so that it can be explained.
- Use the analysis plan to drive the weighting schema. If you need to aggregate by country, use measures to adjust for the lack of representativeness.

What parameters do you use for weighting?

Normally, the preferred weighting for CE is revenue—either the revenue attributed to your own company or overall marketplace revenue. Thus we can say that Citi and companies like it are 15 times more important to an IT vendor than Dow Chemicals (example only) and thus should be weighted 15 times. Thus if Citi and others of their ilk have an average CE score of 8, and the much smaller companies have an average of 4, then the average is not 6 but closer to 8.

The problem of small sample size and large weights

If you have fewer than 50 data points in any one cell, it should be reported with great caution. In fact, many executives may not want it reported at all.

If the data is included in a large data set, care should also be taken to prevent a weight from providing misleading results.

For example, in one CEP we undertook, we found that there were only three completed surveys in Korea, and each had the highest result possible. When we weighted these, it skewed the Asia Pacific data dramatically. We removed them.

Weighting should not be used to manipulate data

While weighting is meant to make the data more representative, it can be manipulated. In one case, despite our protestations, our client changed the weighting parameters several times until the results "proved" the answer that management was looking for.

Significance testing

Significance testing provides an understanding of whether or not different results are statistically different.

For example, if our NPS last year was 28 and this year it was 30, would that be a true improvement, or could it just be a sampling aberration?

Most statistical software for creating tables of data allow for significance testing within the data set. Thus, you can determine if there are differences in the current wave of data between different countries, different customer types, etc. The complexity arises when you need to compare effects over time that require different data sets. Often this needs to be undertaken manually at a cost in time and resources; in addition, it is prone to error.

It is important that the CE team makes clear—in presentations, in replies to queries, and in portals—when the results are within the confidence level and there is no statistically valid difference. In this way management will not be making their decision based on what they believe are differences when in fact these may not be so.

The team needs to decide the level of confidence required—95% is great but 90% is just fine and is used more frequently.

Tracking

One goal of any CEP is to track changes across time. You want to know if the Customer Experience is getting better or getting worse.

As we discussed previously, the CEP can legitimately be conducted once per year over a fairly short timescale. Tracking then is simply comparing the results this year to previous years.

If the CEP is conducted as a continuous program, care must be taken in tracking as there will most likely be aberrations.

In some businesses where there are not significant changes and any differences are due to random volatility, it makes no sense to monitor changes over a short time scale.

> One major software vendor's CEO and senior managers had dashboards that provided data in (more or less) real time so that any significant changes could be detected early and addressed. After some usage of the system, it was decided to use moving averages that dampened out the aberrations but still provided tracking of significant changes.

In addition to aberrations, a number of other factors make tracking difficult.

The first is that to track, we need to be asking exactly the same question(s) to an exactly similar group of customers. In terms of the questions, the broad questions can be kept static over many years, but the detailed questions from which most insight and actions will be driven need to change as the marketplace and company strategy changes. This makes tracking at the detail level impossible.

Tracking can also be difficult if you change data collection methodologies or even agencies. Although data collection is supposed to be consistent, in reality it is not. Each agency's approach is a little different. They may also use different sample sources for competitive, non-client supplied sample. The result will be trying to compare apples and oranges. This factor has also kept vendors from changing their data collection agencies, even if they have greater confidence in another agency.

> One of our prospective clients told us, "We cannot risk getting a different answer from last year. You may be better, but your results will probably be different, and I will have to explain why there is a difference, why you are better, and why I did not use you previously."

When moving from one agency to another or one methodology to another, weighting is sometimes applied while running one program wave in parallel between two agencies. This is not perfect, but it is better than the sudden disjoint or sticking with one agency or methodology when you believe another is better.

> At a luncheon some years ago with a long-standing client for a brand image program, he complimented us by saying that he loved our work since every quarter the results varied only a little from the previous quarter. I was shocked and thought it was a criticism, but he reassured me that the consistency was fundamental to what he needed.

Grouping unlike things

"Let's look at the emerging markets. Give me a set of data that combines China, India, Brazil, and Russia." This is easy to do by combining the data but very misleading since these markets are all very different.

There can be a basic problem with the arithmetic mean. If China answers mainly 6/7 out of 10 and Russia answers 1 or 2, we might conclude that emerging markets are 3 or 4 using the average. This is arithmetically accurate but misleading.

Analytics, big data, and predictive modeling

The simplest analysis of data collected from the CEP is undertaken by the use of cross tabulations. An aggregation of the answers from the research is presented cut by various categories (e.g., tiers of customers, geography, industry). This will usually present the average (arithmetic mean), the median (the middle value of the data set), and the mode (most common value). Often these will be similar, but a difference may show that the data is not distributed along the expected bell-shaped curve. Indicators will be found in the tabulations setting out values that are statistically different. For example, China may have a statistically different mean than the United States.

This data can be easily interpreted and presented in a PowerPoint chart deck.

However, certain answers will not be obvious from this analysis. What is driving the CE Index scores? Are a number of the attributes highly correlated, and are we measuring the same aspect (multicollinearity)? Can we predict what will happen if certain aspects of the CE attributes are improved?

A body of mathematics has been developed that provides the tools to get at these underlying aspects of CE. Most of these revolve around driver analysis and predictive modeling.

A number of consulting firms have used these tools to develop specialized, proprietary models that address aspects of the issues. While these may be "sexy" and sound like the "silver bullet," each has been developed for a specific situation, and each has "secret" algorithms that provide the result. As such, they comprise a "black box" that executive management may have a hard time buying in to. It will certainly be difficult to explain, particularly if the result does not match the common sense that the executives have about the subject.

We have found that each situation is unique and a custom approach is better. We use the standard tool set—regression, correlation, and structured equation modeling—to develop the driver analysis that explains the impact of the various attributes on the final outcome—the CE Index.

Analytics

Analytics should, however, be an important part of a Customer Experience Program because they allow sense to be made of large amounts of attribute-rating and satisfaction data by uncovering patterns within that data. The goal is often to provide insight into how different elements of the Customer Experience drive customer satisfaction, choice, or other outcomes that are also measured in the research (e.g., recommending a company to others). Used in this way, analytics can aid decisions about corporate priorities by identifying what attributes of the experience are most important to customers and on which ones a company should focus its resources to improve or maintain.

One approach to assessing the Customer Experience a company provides is to simply look at summary measures such as "top box" or means across an array of performance attributes. That technique draws attention to those attributes where performance is lowest overall or versus competitors. It also places all attributes on equal footing in terms of importance to the overall Customer Experience, which is not how customers see things. Instead, some attributes are more important than others, and customers may in fact be willing to "forgive" low performance on an unimportant attribute. Decision makers want to identify what matters most.

You could simply ask customers to tell you in a survey how important each attribute is (usually on some kind of rating scale). This is referred to as "stated importance." There are three often-voiced shortcomings to this approach. First, it is said that customers don't know what is important to them because they act more irrationally than rationally—although in practice, frankly, customers usually do know what's important to them, particularly for rational B2B decisions, and that objection is probably raised more times than it warrants. A more serious limitation is the fact that many times, all attributes will be rated as highly important, so it is not possible to discriminate meaningfully across them and understand where the priorities lie. (Asking customers to rank attributes is not the answer—it is both time-consuming in a survey and unwieldy when the number of attributes gets higher than five, which it almost always will.) Finally, in stating their importance, customers rate certain "cost of entry attributes" as highly important (because cost of entry attributes are important—e.g., "safety" on domestic airline flights), but those are not the attributes that drive satisfaction or vendor choice, which is what we are most concerned about identifying. This is not to say that stated importance is an invalid measure—it is a valid measure of what customers think is important. But it may not identify which attributes are the ones that determine choice.

Analytics can help. The attributes that determine choice can be identified with "driver analysis" techniques that derive measures of importance by examining (statistically) how attribute scores move up and down in tandem with outcomes like satisfaction or vendor choice. This "derived importance" is the strength of the association between the attribute ratings of a company and satisfaction (or other outcomes) with that company, and is generally more indicative than stated importance of which attributes drive choice. Different analytic techniques exist to derive importance, and they may not always be in agreement, to the bewilderment of decision makers. The key to understanding how they differ, and which best fits needs, is how they treat the relationships among the attributes themselves.

One derived importance measure is the correlation coefficient, which indicates the strength of association between individual attributes and outcomes of interest. Correlations are easy to produce, being available in most spreadsheet packages. They are also easy to interpret, going from -1 (if the association is absolutely in the opposite direction, where high scores on the attribute are always associated with low scores on the outcome) to +1, which indicates that the attribute is directly and exactly linked to the outcome.

While it is tempting to use correlations (and they are used often), two shortcomings make these approaches unadvisable. First, correlations do not take into account relationships among the attributes, which could lead to the importance of an attribute being overstated if that attribute is strongly associated with what *really* determines choice. For example, a vendor of consulting services may find that "industry expertise" is an important driver of satisfaction, but that may be due to that attribute's relationship to some other, more important attribute such as "can analyze the most complex business challenges." A correlation-based analysis might put those two attributes on equal footing (and often does a poor job discriminating across multiple attribute sets).

Other approaches based on multiple-regression examine attributes as a set to identify their unique influence on an outcome variable while taking into account the other attributes. Complications still arise when attributes are related to each other (called "multicollinearity"), as they often are in driver analysis involving several attributes. It becomes hard to tease out what's important when the different attributes represent overlapping concepts, such as "understands your business needs" and "understands your industry."

More advanced modeling techniques, such as structural equation modeling and principal components regression, attempt to get around this condition by identifying broader dimensions represented by those overlapping attributes—essentially placing them into groups—and then identifying how important those *dimensions* are in driving the outcome in question. While those dimension-based models may in fact do a better job representing reality, they are less palatable in large organizations where people or business units are responsible for individual attributes and want to understand the unique contribution of each one—regardless of whether or not it overlaps with other attributes. Other techniques with names like "relative weight analysis" and "average over orderings regression" are designed to identify that unique impact of an individual attribute. These can represent good compromises and have grown in popularity in recent years.

Communicating analytics

No matter what technique you choose, when communicating results to executives, be sure to focus less on the tools and statistics (no matter how impressive they sound) and more on portraying the relationships they describe in an intuitive way. An array of Greek letters and complex labels may look impressive, but if the results and their implications are not easy to understand—and quickly—they will be ignored.

Results can be communicated effectively with numbers that have an intuitive interpretation, by, for example, assigning a relative weight to each attribute that corresponds to its importance. In the example below, the weights are based on a (hypothetical) model and have been proportioned to 100%. Overall cost and overall value are three times as important as having nationally known experts on staff, and twice as important as a responsive account team.

Attribute	Impact
Overall cost	18%
Overall quality	18%
Solutions that fit business needs	14%
First to market with new innovations	12%
Commitment to your business objectives	11%
Responsive account team	9%
Post sales support	7%
Nationally-known experts on staff	6%
Industry expertise	5%

Another way to portray the results is by graphing impact importance against performance vs. competitors (e.g., your mean score minus their mean score). The "leverage" chart below plots importance (on the vertical axis) against performance (on the horizontal axis) in just that way, providing an intuitive summary of performance against competitors and implications for the outcome under study. It shows:

- High-priority weaknesses to fix: attributes important to customers where performance lags competitors
- Low-priority weaknesses to fix: attributes less important to customers where performance lags competitors
- Strengths to emphasize in communications or sales discussions: those attributes most important to customers in which your performance leads the competition
- Strengths to maintain: those attributes less important to customers but where your performance leads the competition

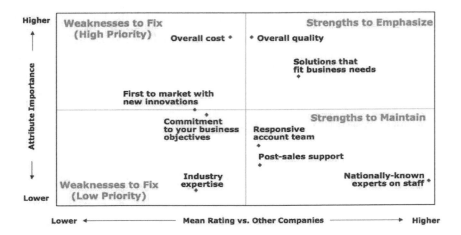

Communications about results are especially compelling if they describe the relationship between performance on particular attributes and business outcomes. Statements that tie movement in an attribute to a financial outcome such as share of wallet—for example, "catching up to Competitor X on Attribute Y will increase our share of wallet across customers by 3%"—grab attention.

At the beginning of this chapter, we talked of "garbage in, garbage out," and sound data is even more important if it is being used with analytics. Analytics will deliver value only if they are based on high-quality data—data that is reliable, from questions that are clear, and from appropriate respondents who are paying attention and motivated to take the survey. It is difficult to spot meaningful relationships in low-quality data; there is too much noise and it is hard to discern the patterns. (And, of course, low-quality data runs the risk of providing information that is simply incorrect.) That's why good analytics are based on a foundation of reliable data, and the first step in any analysis is looking at different measures of data quality and suitability for analysis. And analytics cannot, ever, make up for bad data. "Statistical fixes" don't work.

Reporting

A basic output from data collection and analysis is the report.

The norm today is a PowerPoint deck, or decks, with the highlights of the program results:

- The CE Index
- CE Index compared with a previous time period
- CE Index compared with CE Indexes for competitors
- Breakdown of the CE components
- Assessment of various attributes:
  - Aspects regarded as important
  - Touch points
  - Roles
  - Product groups
- Areas of strength
- Areas of weakness
- Actions required to correct areas of weakness

The report is usually developed and presented at the most senior level and subsequently is "sliced and diced" to provide a similar format for product groups, geographic regions and/or countries, touch points, etc.

This can run to several thousand pages of report, each with results that need to be checked, that need significant testing, and perhaps that need moving averages calculated. This is a huge and costly affair and one that takes a considerable amount of time. And it is likely that several thousand of the pages will never be looked at by anyone.

A little knowledge is a dangerous thing

We have come across many instances where members of our client's staff want to have access to the data.

> *Just give me the data and an analysis tool. That way, I can just slice and dice" it myself.*

Usually the people who request this are smart people, but often they do not have the experience or knowledge that allows them to stay out of trouble. Some examples of this are set out below:

> "The answers I get are different from the CEP team's." – The staff member used unweighted data.

> "The data says that 85% of our customers overall want a faster delivery time." – Actually the question was only asked of the people that said delivery was an issue – 23%.

> "We are much better now than a year ago." – Actually there was no significant difference between the two results.

Our strong recommendation is to have the data held only by the CEP team and to have them (or their research partner) undertake the analysis work as *ad hoc* queries.

Dashboards

An alternative approach is to use a permissioned portal that creates custom reports and displays them on demand, provided the requester is authorized to access these.

These are often called "dashboards" and likened to that in a motor vehicle. The concept is that the data will be available in real time to allow executive management to view the continually changing Customer Experience and take actions accordingly.

This can work well in a B2C setting.

Some years back, we developed (but did not implement) a system for Sears based on in-store kiosks so that customers were incented to undertake a simple satisfaction questionnaire about their experiences when in the store. The concept was that the data would be collected and analyzed in real time and the results displayed on a dashboard in a war room in Chicago. Management would monitor stores across the country for emerging trends and systemic issues.

For B2B, the situation is different. Even in the most comprehensive program, there are unlikely to be more than 100 interviews each day. Observing this in real time would be like watching paint dry.

In the B2B context, although we may call it a dashboard, the solution is really a permissioned portal with results that are updated periodically and held static until the next update. The weighting and significance testing is included dynamically in the model.

The thousands of PowerPoint charts can be replaced by this permissioned portal. Let's say that the general manager of Spain in your company wants to access Spain's results. He logs on, and the portal gives him permission to access Spanish data (and probably comparative data for total Europe and globally) but, perhaps, not data for Germany. The portal will present the base data but should also allow the GM to "drill down" within his country data: "Wow, our overall CE Index has fallen since last quarter. Why? Is it a regional issue within Spain? Is it a problem with certain industries?"

Dashboards need to be constructed well and provide insight to executive management in an easy-to-use and pleasing display. Too often, the graphic designers go too far and provide something that looks "nifty" but does not convey the insight well. An example is the use of 3D charts, which can be misleading.

The CEP team needs to work with the designer to develop chart styles that work well. The development of the portal and its supporting data set is not an easy or inexpensive task. However, the cost and time to develop the alternative PowerPoint decks can easily offset this, providing executive management has bought in to the approach.

One challenge is reacting to changes in organization structure or customer segments. The portal needs to be easy to alter to accommodate these changes.

Non-survey approaches

While a survey-based approach will yield a robust quantitative result that can be "sliced and diced" to allow insight and action, there are a lot of other aspects to CE that can be achieved independently.

We recommend a customer audit as part of this. In a customer audit, either members of the vendor or an outside consultant plays at being a customer and goes through the experiences that a customer would have. At the simplest level, he might use a telephone number from the website to access customer service. The passage through the IVR system, the ability of either the system or the operators to resolve the issue, etc. is observed and reported back so improvements can be made.

Many years ago, Intuit, the software company, used a "follow-home" approach. When a customer purchased their Quicken software, a member of the company would request to come back with the customer and observe how they installed and used the software. Improvements were spotted in the documentation and the user experience, and changes were made.

One CEO calls his company switchboard once or twice a week and counts the number of rings before it is answered.

One key to this approach is that it should not be a single-shot operation but should be structured to be part of a continuous operation—part of the CEP.

Social media as a method for data collection

Social media can be a valuable touch point as set out in Chapter 10. Increasingly, companies are turning to social media to collect data about their customers and their experiences.

However, measuring customer satisfaction is not easy. In the past few years, numerous social media tools have popped up, promising to track and measure customer satisfaction in real time and effectively. But social media certainly does not give you the whole picture—not all your customers are on social media. A recent RONIN IT Pulse survey shows that the majority of business and IT professionals do not use social media such as Facebook and Twitter for professional purposes. You can use social media tools to measure the effectiveness of your latest content campaign, detect customer-service issues, and uncover brand issues, but those can solve only part of the puzzle when it comes to measuring customer satisfaction.

In one case, a client undertook an analysis of web-based "mentions" of their company and whether the comments were favorable or not. The problem here was that they had no way of knowing who the individuals were who had made the comments. It was likely that some of these were their customers, but no one could be sure and the results could not be verified.

In some cases, a "closed community" can be developed and used for text analytics on comments, blogs, etc., and this at least narrows down the response base to more known individuals.

15: ACTIONS

All the work so far has been to get to this point. It seems obvious, but for a CEP to have any value, it must lead to actions that will either resolve problems with the Customer Experience or improve an already great Customer Experience to achieve even greater success.

This all sounds very obvious, but so many of the CEPs and customer satisfaction programs out there fall short on this. Often the program is seen more as a scorecard:

- A scorecard to understand current position:
    - "We have a B+ this year."
- A scorecard to track results over time:
    - "We had a B- last year and this year we have a B."
- A scorecard to determine competitive position:
    - "Although we improved from B- to B, our main competitor also improved from a B+ to and A."

If you get an A, perhaps you can relax and move on, but even then you are missing the opportunity to do even better. Lower scores, particularly if they are worse than your competitors, require a fix … and the fix requires action.

Taking action is the mother lode of a CEP. Without action, the program is nothing more than a scorecard and will likely do more harm than good. You have asked a customer if there are any problems and they have said "yes." And then you do nothing. This is where a CEP can cause even more dissatisfaction in the customer base.

The outputs from the measurement phase are set out in the previous chapter and include:

- Threshold alerts – the customer's answer(s) imply that there is a (fairly) acute problem. The alert goes to the sales representative and probably his/her manager. For an individual issue, it can be acted on promptly. If this is happening with multiple customers, the issue must be flagged as a systemic issue and referred to relevant management. The sales representative should still be alerted and can use the alert to find out more details regarding the problem than came from the measurement instrument.

  The CEP team should be on the lookout for similar alerts that demonstrate they are probably systemic and flag them as such, alerting the sales representative and manager that the issue is broader and will be addressed separately.

- Individual data accessible for each customer contact who was interviewed – this is similar to the threshold-alert data above but does not require immediate action. It is used to analyze individual responses and responses from different roles in a specific account.

- Analysis of the measurement data – the data shows that many customers share the same problem. The dashboard might also display the problem, and the associated "drill down" may pinpoint where the problem is.

Steps in implementing actions – problem categorization into "individual" and "systemic"

Actions required will depend on what the issues are that the measurement phase uncovers. They can be classified into two states in each of two variables. People seem to love quadrant charts, so here is one:

The first (x axis) shows whether the issue is an individual one or one that points to a systemic problem. If the customer just does not like the salesperson, it is an individual problem. If the customers in general find the time of delivery for their orders is too lengthy, this is a more systemic problem.

The second dimension (y axis) relates to whether the issue can be solved in the short term or whether it requires a more strategic/longer-term solution. The delivery issue may be able to be solved immediately by switching to a speedier carrier. Changing the sales representative may also be easy and not very costly to do. If there are problems with the ease of use of the product, this could require a major product redesign, which could be both lengthy and costly to correct.

For most problems, getting the fix quickly is important. If measurement takes place only once a year, and if it takes a month or two to distribute the results, the likelihood of a solution being developed and implemented within an 18-month time scale from when the problem arose is low. In the current day, 18 months is unacceptably long. The type of industry in terms of "life of product" will help determine the frequency of the measurement. Continuous rather than yearly is probably best for most industries today.

There is a need for establishing an issues database where issues can be logged into each category, a problem owner identified, and resolution tracked. This database should also allow issues that arise from other sources to be logged (e.g., complaints to the sales representative, online complaints, etc.).

It seems logical to address the simple and inexpensive fixes informally. This is fine provided there is no cross impact that will affect other issues. In one case we saw a situation where delivery times were cut, but the solution adopted was to skimp on the product testing before delivery, which caused even greater problems.

In the ideal situation, all problems can be easily rectified, but this is rarely the case. In most cases, there needs to be a trade-off between resolving different issues and assessing the optimal portfolio of resolution—the best bang for the buck.

Prioritization of issues

Having categorized the issues, decisions need to be made as to which of the systemic issues should be addressed first. Analysis can be undertaken to divide these by tier.

In the example below, we have set up a framework for this. If we are concentrating on only our Tier 1 customers, we should focus on the issues that affect these most—in the example, Issue 4. But there are other aspects we might take into account: The Tier 2 customer set has a marketplace opportunity and a margin that is higher than just considering today's revenue. In this case, focus on Issue 3 may be more useful.

Optimizing Resolution

Customer Set	Revenue	Market Opportunity	% of total revenue margin	% of population with the problem			
				Issue #1	Issue #2	Issue #3	Issue #4
Tier 1	80%	50%	60%	23%	10%	29%	50%
Tier 2	15%	30%	38%	40%	15%	42%	4%
Tier 3	5%	20%	2%	70%	10%	65%	12%
	100%	100%	100%				

Having established the priority for fixing the issues, we should now consider the options for doing so and the cost of the change.

Identifying the root cause

Identifying the problem is just the first step to rectifying it.

The next part of the "drill down" is to get to the "what is needed to fix the problem." The first step requires in-depth interviews with a small number of the discontented customers. If a pattern emerges quickly, you can stop the interviews. If not, a more extensive investigation may be needed. You should also put the question to your salespeople and others who interact with your customers.

Next, you need to understand the root cause(s) of each issue.

- Develop the timeline of the issue.
- What were the factors that directly caused the issue?

- What could have been differently that would have resolved the issue?
- What are the alternatives that would resolve the issue?
- What side effects would the various alternatives have?
- How sustainable would each alternative be?

Exploration of alternative solutions

Not all the alternatives will result in a total solution, so each alternative solution should be assessed for:

- Value
- Cost

Then a simple model can be used to determine the "biggest bang for the buck." With each alternative scenario of resolution, what will each cost and what can we expect to be the result as measured by the CE score? This will largely be guesswork, but usually several alternatives fall out easily, and the model is used just to document our rationale for deciding on the final action that will be taken. It provides a framework for the decision.

Customer Experience Alternatives

Touch point:	Web site		
Importance:	8.3		
Current assessment:	6.2		
Target assessment:	8		

Scenario:	Cost	Point gain	Cost/point
A	3.6	0.04	90.0
B	5	0.4	12.5
C	10	0.6	16.7
D	12	0.8	15.0
E	15	1.2	12.5

For long-term issues (and if time permits), the various options being considered could be included in the next round of the CE survey but filtered so that only the people who raised the issue are asked their preference for the different approaches to resolving the issue. This provides solid feedback to management and also adds to the customer's comfort level that something is being done to resolve the issue and their advice is being taken into account in the decision.

After the action has been implemented, the customers who had the issues should be notified. If implementation is going to take considerable time, you should inform the customers that "we listened, we developed a resolution, and we should have this implemented in XX weeks."

Finally, when the implementation is complete, we need to monitor it for effectiveness. The next round of data collection can be used for this.

16: FEEDBACK TO CUSTOMERS

Let's imagine I am a senior executive in one of your largest customers. I receive an email asking me to take a web survey. A few things have not been going well in the relationship, so I am pleased to take the survey and communicate my concerns.

The interview seems long and asks about a lot of attributes that do not seem very relevant. I then get to the areas where I have had problems. I answer these negatively.

I complete the survey but never hear back as to whether anything will be done to correct the issues. I feel more dissatisfied than before I started the survey.

We ask customers if they are satisfied, and if not, what the problem is. This takes up their time but offers significant value to the vendor. Whether the vendor is going to take any action or not is not the point. The point is that there needs to be feedback to the customer.

Anyone in sales knows that the only way to win continuing business is through a continuous dialog. Again a standard sales technique is to coax out the objections and then deal with them. If the CEP coaxes out the problem but then the customer is ignored, there is a feeling of abandonment.

Why not send an email back saying, "We heard you. We shall look into the matter and get back to you within one week (or some other time period)"? Then a week later, you send another email setting out your findings and what the company is doing about them.

Too often I have heard: "The customers always complain, and we do not have the resources to fix the problems." Even so, ignoring the problems will do no good. Better to fess up and go back to the customer with, "We accept your criticism and have looked into how to rectify it. Unfortunately correcting this will take time and resources. At the moment other areas have been given higher priority, so we cannot do this immediately. I shall communicate with you in three months to inform you of our progress."

We undertook a pilot for one major software company that was successful in collecting the data required. However, as they looked into the comments, they realized that they had a lot to do to correct some major issues. Rather than go out to their entire customer base, collect the criticisms, and then not be able to respond, they decided to postpone the program until they were better placed to respond. It was not the best solution, but it was a recognition that raising the issues and then being unable to correct them was probably more damaging than to not raise the issues.

The Customer Connection approach, set out in the appendix, uses a real-time approach to the initial reply as well as inclusion of updates in the continuous, personalized dialog.

17: WHY SOME PROGRAMS FAIL

Customer Experience Programs are complex and all-embracing for a company. If they work well, they can fundamentally support the company strategy and become a structural asset for the company.

However, many programs are started as the group in charge of customer satisfaction studies attempts to shift to a more strategic role. Often they do not realize the pitfalls, and often these programs fail. They may be totally discredited, or in the face of political and organizational headwinds, they may revert to a simple customer satisfaction program.

We have seen several hundred customer satisfaction approaches that have attempted to step up to fully fledged Customer Experience Programs. Some have succeeded; some have failed.

There are nine most common reasons we have found for failure:

1. Not enough commitment from the top
2. "Opt out" by lower levels of management/staff
3. A focus on cost reduction, which eats into CE initiatives
4. A focus on the "scorecard" and not the actions
5. Attempting a total solution from the beginning, which can be too complex

6. Not "staying the course" – often executive management are seduced by the latest "shiny thing" and lose interest in the CEP, which is a multiyear program
7. Adopting a "packaged" consumer-based program that does not fit the vendors B2B model
8. Defaulting into a formula-based customer satisfaction program
9. Inability to measure value found

Let's look at each of these:

Not enough commitment from the top

As we have set out in previous chapters, the CEP will be most optimal when it is a fundamental part of a company's strategy and is used as a competitive differentiator. This will not happen unless the concept is totally embraced by the CEO.

If the CEO pays lip service to CE but does not drive its company-wide acceptance, it is very likely to fail.

"Opt out" by lower levels of management/staff

Even if the CEO is fully behind a CEP, lower levels of management often just do not buy in. Often their rewards structure is very short term and oriented toward revenue and profit growth; these drivers can be in conflict with providing an excellent, longer-term Customer Experience.

The CEO must lead the implementation of a reward system that matches the CE objectives. This will tend to be longer in term than the traditional, and it needs to be overlaid on the short-term objectives that companies use to manage their businesses.

A focus on cost reduction, which eats into CE initiatives

Even when the CEP is functioning well, it is usually regarded as a cost despite its contribution to profitability. As such, if the company embarks on a cost-cutting cycle, it is not uncommon for the CEP budget to be reduced to show cost savings. In addition, some of the initiatives to drive improvements in the Customer Experience will also be curtailed, and management may step back from measurement systems that are likely to show degradation owing to these other cost cuts.

CEP is a long-term program in which cost is likely to outweigh value in the early few years; however, it will more than make up for this across the longer term. Some companies have the stomach for this; others do not. And others come on harder times that prompt a pragmatic approach to radical cost reduction, including in the CEP.

Focus on "scorecard" not actions

A CEP provides value through the actions that are prompted to improve CE in a cost-effective manner.

If the CEP is used only as a scorecard for management presentations, and perhaps management haranguing, the value will be limited, and sooner or later, the program will be cut or reduced in size, scope, and budget to match this limited use.

Attempting a total solution from the beginning

Implementing a CEP is a big deal requiring a lot of management commitment, a significant cost, and a change of culture to embrace the concept and the results.

While there can be a drive for urgency, the implementation of this type of program cannot be rushed and needs an extensive pilot. The implementation needs to be partial at first and then extended. Attempting a total solution from scratch invites disaster as several companies have found out.

Not "staying the course"

Executive management in companies is confronted with a lot of issues on an ongoing basis—not the least of which is the set of quarterly results. Many of the abilities of a successful CEO have to do with being able to switch from one subject to another rapidly without missing a beat.

Most can develop both vision and strategies and stick with them until they show they are not working—and then move to an alternative. Others are always being lured by the "next big thing."

A CEP requires senior executive support over an extended period, and some CEOs who were enthusiastic at the beginning lose interest over time as other issues seem more exciting or more valuable.

Beyond the CEO, there are typically some (or many) executives who are champions for the CEP. They see the value and fully support it. If these executives leave or move to other jobs where the CEP has a lesser impact, the momentum can be lost.

Adopting a "packaged" consumer-based program

There are dozens of consulting groups offering prepackaged CEPs. These offer a quick, cheap way of implementing a program supported by executive-friendly graphics and dashboards.

These are also typically addressed to B2C companies.

While these may offer a reasonable solution, they typically do not address the unique issues in each company as detailed previously in this book, and they often fail.

Adopting such an approach fails in two ways. Firstly, the investment in the prepackaged approach is lost. Secondly, and more important, the approach is often discredited, and the opportunity of "getting it right" is lost. In companies where we have seen this, the failure also discredits the concept overall, making it impossible to introduce an alternative CEP for many years while the wounds heal.

Defaulting into a formula-based customer satisfaction program

Customer satisfaction organizations within the company often strive for greater recognition and can "re-brand" a regular customer satisfaction program as a CEP.

While a sound customer satisfaction program is an excellent base for a CEP, the CEP goes a lot further in terms of value and scope.

In one case, a CEO was expecting a full CEP and felt cheated when it turned out to be a rehash of their previous customer satisfaction program.

Inability to measure value found

Customer Experience is somewhat like advertising. Management is always asking for quantifiable benefits from advertising and other marketing efforts, but these are invariably spurious. The sales process is just too long and complex to allow attribution of specific sales to specific marketing touches, particularly in a B2B environment. The CEP scorecard shows improvement or not against competition, but there are too many other variables to measure increased revenues or profits that have been caused by the CEP.

At a macro level, Bain and Company—and other companies using the NPS approach—have spent lots of time and effort linking high NPS to company performance. There certainly seems to be a correlation, but whether the high NPS is a driver of great performance or whether companies with great performance tend to have a better Customer Experience is less clear.

The CEP concept implies changes that are prompted by data derived from customers to provide a better Customer Experience. This in turn translates into value.

The most successful approaches rely on the acceptance of the "overall high value" from CEP and then the development of tangible goals that can be measured.

In many cases, this equates to high NPS scores, and that is just fine. Others include high response rates to the measurement survey—with sales staff rewarded not just on the scores of their accounts but the numbers of these that responded.

Without targets and a measurement of success in achieving these, the CEP is likely to have less impact and may not be renewed from year to year. If management does not set the targets, the CEP team must do so.

18: ROADMAP FOR THE CEP

In the last chapter, one of the causes of failure was attempting to move too rapidly to a complete solution. The CEP, as we continue to stress, is not easy, and it requires a measured approach with interim checkpoints to achieve the full system than we are hoping for.

In some dictatorial companies, the CEO may be able to say, "This is the way I want it. Do it." But this is rare and normally the CEO needs to lay out the vision and have management buy in to it with vigor. As we have set out in Part 2, there are a lot of corporate cultural aspects to be implemented, in addition to incorporating the CE mentality into both corporate and product-level strategy.

There is also a lot of up-front work to design the most relevant framework.

This is why a roadmap needs to be developed (and followed) for a phased implementation, with each step reinforcing the concept and building support.

Roadmap

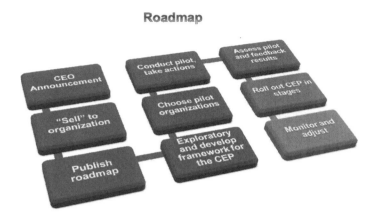

Even before Step 1, the CEO must have embraced the concept fully. If not, do not bother attempting a full-blown CEP. Use a lower-impact customer satisfaction program.

Step 1 – The CEO Announcement

The CEO needs to announce the program and show very clearly that it is a fundamental part of the vision and strategy. This announcement needs to be reinforced in every company communication, meeting, and workshop. Organizational structure changes that are needed to implement the approach should be hinted at but not decided on or implemented until later in the rollout.

Step 2 – Selling to the Organization

Initial selling must be to the CEO's direct reports and then farther down the line. Objections (as in other selling situations) should be encouraged, put on the table, debated, and then refuted.

The selling should continue throughout the rollout and beyond, but it should start at this point and continue when the roadmap has been developed, the pilot selected, and then when feedback on pilot results is prepared.

In the background, the roadmap with the steps, timings, and resources required should be developed. At this stage some preliminary goals and measurement parameters should also be developed; these may be modified later.

Step 3 – Publish the Roadmap

Publishing the roadmap is a simple step, but it lays out the plan for getting to the CEP. It not only puts people on notice that the plan will be implemented, it also establishes the expectations—and we all know that managing expectations is the key to success.

Timelines should be generous, and the intent should be to implement faster than the timeline rather than having tight timelines and being forced to deliver late.

The CEO will push for fast timelines, but it is key for the CEP team to push back and convince the CEO that if things are rushed, there is a greater risk of issues arising.

The roadmap should be used as a guideline communication vehicle and should be updated regularly, showing success against targets. The aim is to keep the roadmap alive and use it as a PR vehicle for the program.

Step 4 – Explore and Develop CEP Framework

As we have set out in Parts 2 and 3, there is a lot of preparatory work needed:

- Building a customer database
- Incorporating the CE aspect into corporate strategy and product strategy and tactics
- Definition of appropriate:
  - Product/service categories
  - Customer sets
  - Customer roles
  - Touch points
  - Customer journey and life cycle

It is also important at this time to plan the transition from the current customer satisfaction program to the CEP. This may require organizational and staff changes.

In planning for the implementation phase, the current customer satisfaction approach should be reviewed and changes made to it to reflect the differences. It may require different methodologies and approaches (e.g., a telephone-based survey for Tier 1 customers). The additional roles may require a different approach to acquiring sample.

You also need to develop the cost estimates and value hypotheses (e.g., "Cost is 15% more than the current customer satisfaction study, but if overall Customer Experience can be raised from the current level by 10%, we can expect the retention cost to fall by $X and the sales per customer to increase by $Y.").

Step 5 – Select Pilot

A full rollout will take a long time and require the CEO's "act of faith" to continue for that time period. It is best to find some "low-hanging fruit" and implement a pilot project. This can be done more quickly, allowing results to be shown. It also does not over stretch the CEP team by creating higher risk.

Selection of the pilot is fundamental. It should be an area that is regarded as most important and one that is less complex than others. It should be on one of the following dimensions:

- Customer individuals
- Touch points
- Products
- Phase in life cycle

Most companies tackle a particular product dimension; however, this can be suboptimal since there are so many "fixes" that are more generic. It may be easier and more effective to tackle a <u>touch point</u> across a variety of products that also avoids the NIH syndrome.

Ideally this matches with the overall strategic positioning (e.g., highest quality, best customer service).

Coupled with the project itself are its goals. These should be established with metrics so that both the program cost and the results from the successful implementation can be easily measured and presented.

People's attention spans these days are short, so target the pilot to be completed within three months.

Step 6 – Conduct the Pilot

After the framework has been decided, a research project needs to be conducted to gather pertinent data to assess the pilot environment and to establish actions that can be used to rectify any problem areas.

In one touch-point-oriented pilot, we focused on the customer-service call center. We used a simple web survey with current customer contacts to assess the experience. The NPS question version was, "Would you recommend … based on your experience using the Vendor A customer-service center?" There were also a number of drill-down questions related to the IVR system, wait time, ability of the agent to answer their questions, attitude of the agent, etc.

Finally, an open-ended response was requested: "How can we do better?"

The customer-service center for the pilot was just one of several and used English language only.

The results were assembled and analyzed, and a set of possible actions determined. A short workshop was called that addressed the various possible actions and the cost of implementing them.

A few in-depth interviews were conducted with individuals who had raised a lot of issues, and they were asked if the planned changes were made, how those changes would alter their score. Also, they were asked which of the actions would give the vendor the "best bang for the buck" in their eyes?

This took the first six weeks, and subsequently the actions were agreed and implemented. At week 10 of the pilot, the survey was conducted again, and the improved scores became part of a report indicating the value from such a CEP program.

For the CEP team it is important to widely show the results, have the CEO endorse them, and then sell the results to others in the organization.

The team should also channel results to the PR department and the media. It is hard to stop an acclaimed success.

There is always a risk of things not working as expected, so it is probably sound to determine an exit strategy if things go wrong, such as:

- The CEO changes his/her mind.
- There is too much push back from the ranks.
- There are too many operational issues.
- There is not enough payback.

Step 7 – Roll Out Program

When the sign-offs are in place, implement the rest of the CEP in logical phases (as established in Step 3 and perhaps revised based on the results of the pilot).

Step 8 – Monitor and Adjust

Nothing stands still. Even if the program is a resounding success, it will need continuous monitoring and adjustment over time. Customer sets will be re-aligned, new products will be added, others will be dropped, and certain touch points will become more or less important.

19: CONCLUSION

The ultimate CEP is far-reaching, and although we have been involved in most of the component parts, no one company has implemented all parts and integrated them together.

The benefits are obvious: true alignment with the customer makes sense, and many studies have sought (with varying levels of success) to correlate high Customer Experience levels with overall corporate results.

Competitive differentiation is possible through a sound CEP in a world where differentiation through other means can be transient.

The journey is just starting for many companies while some are well on their way. I can promise that the effort is worth it.

But I can also promise ... it's not that easy.

APPENDIX

APPENDIX: A "CUSTOMER CONNECTION" PROGRAM – BEYOND CUSTOMER EXPERIENCE

Introduction

The Customer Connection Program is an approach that allows a personalized interaction between customers and their vendor. It fulfills many of the aspects of a Customer Experience Program but also encompasses a vehicle for conducting other research with customers and even selling products and services.

If you could afford it, you would have a team of courteous, experienced staff enjoy an ongoing, face-to-face dialog with each of your customers—selling them upgrades, cross selling your product range, checking to see if your marketing messages are working, getting their suggestions for improvements, and telling them about what is happening in your company—specifically what you have done to respond to their requests and gauging their overall satisfaction with the relationship.

Most companies cannot afford this, particularly for their non-Tier 1 customers. They need an approach that can complement what you can do face-to-face. The Customer Connection Program is a "personalized," web-based relationship and loyalty approach that provides that complement.

The Customer Connection Program (CCP)

Winning new customers is just the starting point. Fundamental to success is retaining and growing those customers that provide greatest profitability. This depends on understanding which are the best customers and then maintaining a sound relationship with them.

Customer relationships depend on a linkage between the vendor and the customer that was traditionally undertaken by experienced, courteous sales and service personnel. In today's environment the need is even greater, but cost and availability pressures limit how much can be done in the traditional way.

RONIN has implemented a unique Customer Connection Program (CCP) that offers an affordable alternative that:

- Enables one-to-one marketing
- Allows a personalized supply of information to each customer
- Allows testing of marketing messages
- Collects wants and needs
- Gauges reaction to new products, price changes, etc.

And it accomplishes all of this while increasing retention and customer growth through behavior-based cross selling. It also alerts management on a personal, customer level (e.g., "This customer is likely to buy from a competitor") to aggregated data to address systemic problems (e.g., "Few customers have a high regard for our call center service support").

But it goes further than that. The Customer Connection Program (CCP) takes generic feedback from the vendor and personalizes it back to relevant customers in an interactive and personalized dialog.

How does it work? New customers

When a customer buys his first service offering, he/she is sent an email welcoming him to your company and asking if he/she would like to maintain an open line of communication with the company. The customer clicks on a link and is launched into a personalized interaction with your company's CCP. The interaction takes the form of a series of questions and answers with feedback to the customer. Each customer becomes a "member" of the program. The interaction is an entertaining, enjoyable experience, not an interrogation as can be found in many customer satisfaction or other survey approaches. This initial interaction is brief and is aimed at discovering if all is well with the installation of this first product/service. The customer is advised that he/she will be contacted again shortly and a date is set for this.

After the initial interaction a second email is sent on the appointed date, and another interaction is started—Wave 2. This time, there is a dialog about the sales process, how well the sales representative presented your company's story, etc. What competitors were considered? How were they rated? What is important to this individual customer in the relationship? How is it going so far? The CCP also addresses any problems identified in the last interaction. Have they been solved?

The subsequent waves typically take about 10 minutes and occur once every six weeks or so. In addition, there will be situations where you want to advise customers of changes, new products, new pricing, etc., or where you seek their views on a new product concept, etc. A special interaction is initiated, and based on data we have about this customer from their previous interactions or from customer databases, the interaction is personalized.

> For a telecommunications-carrier program, for example, we created dialog with all small/medium business customers about the merits of a new local service offering. A special, bundled price might be offered based on a predictive model of purchasing behavior. If they are of a certain segment type (e.g., technosavvy), they might also be offered Internet service. The dialog emulates what a good salesperson would do—it asks questions based on prior knowledge of the customer and then, based on these answers, make offers. The process is subtle rather than a hard sales pitch and stops short of the "close," allowing that to take place with a sales representative in person or by phone.

When a customer responds with answers that indicate an issue (e.g., he/she is dissatisfied with some aspects of the relationship, he/she is interested in receiving information regarding an upgrade), the appropriate individuals in the vendor organization are notified. If there is a major issue identified as a threshold in the system, an email is sent automatically, in real time, to the appropriate party. When a lesser problem occurs, these are sent in batches with systemic problems identified separately from those of specific individuals. Actions to correct the problems need to be determined and implemented, and feedback about this needs to be sent to the CCP for inclusion in feedback to appropriate customers.

For example, say 200 customers find the speed of response from the customer service organization to be average or below average. Management would be alerted to this and would take steps to improve it. The steps they have taken/are taking are fed back to only these 200 customers at their next interaction, and they are asked if the response time is now better. Even if improvements cannot be made, communication to the customers, giving the reasons and the fact that there are other priorities, is significantly better than no feedback at all, and it builds trust and loyalty.

Although the customer receives the email from your company and interacts through a website with your company's "look and feel," both emails and the interaction are managed by RONIN, requiring little or no IT support from your company and allowing an inexpensive, easy-to-use approach. Some data needs to be downloaded from your customer databases, and the results can be fed back; the interface, however, is simple.

The CCP comprises a set of personalization software based on personal interactions. The questions, the feedback, and the logic are programmed and thereafter operate automatically being updated as issues are uncovered and corrective actions made by the company. The cost to administer the approach to many thousands of customers is not much greater than to a few hundred.

Over time, the dialog becomes a connection, which keeps the customer in contact with the company. The company in turn uses the data at both individual and aggregated levels to improve the relationship through actions. Part of the data analysis is the use of a RONIN model that determines early signs of defection as well as individual customers who are likely candidates for additional or upgraded service offerings and pricing/discounting recommendations.

How does it work? Existing customers

The program is also suitable for current customers, providing them a valuable relationship and loyalty program. Typically, an email is sent to current customers requesting they register for the program. When they do so, they receive the various "waves" of the program that are relevant.

In a recent program, the sign-up rate without active follow-up was nearly 40%.

How we implement the program

We work with your staff in a feasibility study to explore the current customer-relationship approaches, to determine metrics of the existing situation, and to establish goals for the CCP. This takes three to four weeks. Output from this will be a benchmarked analysis of your current program and a detailed analysis of the targets for the CCP program. The payback for the setup of these programs is typically less than three months, and the ongoing program can cost as little as $5 per customer per year—with increased retention and significant "up selling."

Customers who are not web enabled

If some or all of your customers are not web enabled, we offer a call-center option that uses the same approach and script to carry out the Customer Connection from a customer service representative.

Program objectives

The overall objectives of the Customer Connection Program vary by company but typically include collecting information that will enable you to:

- Provide personalized information about your company to the customer
- Sell upgrades, supplies, new products
- Test marketing messages and reactions to new products, pricing, changes in terms, etc.; and to solicit input to these

- Understand customer needs,
- Understand their expectations
- Understand their purchase criteria for your company and its major competitors:
- Measure customer satisfaction and loyalty
- Determine customers' willingness to repurchase and recommend
- Understand customer stated importance of selection criteria
- Determine ratings of the important selection criteria
- Measure brand image and advertising effectiveness
- Determine and track perceived strengths and weaknesses
- Detect early signs of customer defection

Additionally, ad hoc aspects can be covered. For example:

- Three months after a new product is installed, how does the customer rate it?
- A new packaging is introduced. What is the customer reaction?
- Who wants to sign up for a seminar?
- Plans are being made to change the customer support process. What do customers think?
- A new product is being developed. Who wants to be involved in the pilot phase? During this phase, what are their views, reactions?

Information that will be provided to the customer relates only to that which is personally relevant (e.g., if the customer has not purchased a particular product, upgrade information is not relevant but an attempt to cross sell this product might be). Based on the profile of the customer, aspects typically included are:

- Actions being taken to address areas of detected dissatisfaction are set out in the next quarterly interaction, and the customer is asked if these have solved the problem.

- Issues related to products that the customer has purchased—upgrades, new versions, ancillary products/services, "tips and tricks," other customer comments on usage
- Seminars, conferences that have relevance
- Other aspects covered in the "connection" include:
  - How the total customer base feels about certain topics. These results can be set up as an instant poll with results-to-date fed back to each member. The final results would be fed back in the next wave.
  - How this customer is benchmarked against others (e.g., lower usage than others in same industry/size range)

A specific case study version of the Customer Connection approach – the ICON Connection Program

ICON was a Customer Experience Program for a software vendor who wanted to forge a closer relationship with the customers and channel partners of a recently acquired product set.

It was designed to achieve numerous objectives:

- Provide a cost-effective means of communicating with customers and channel partners
- Stem the defection of customers to competitors
- Provide a mechanism for introducing companion products to those already in use by the customer/channel partner
- Offer a means for customers and channel partners to provide feedback directly to the product team
- Provide access to such items as white papers and technical information

All communications were personalized and made specific to the individual's environment and interest areas.

How it works

The program was rolled out worldwide with the system translated into French, Italian, German, Spanish, Chinese, Japanese, Korean, Brazilian Portuguese, and Russian. Because each geographic region used different marketing approaches, provision was made for localization of each of the dialogs.

Facts and figures

- Initial registrations exceeded 40%.
- 56% of these members returned for Dialog 2, and after 10 rounds of dialog, the return rate was still averaging nearly 50%.
- 10% of the members requested follow-up through the "contact me" buttons.
  - Some of these potential prospects were rated as qualified and have resulted in early sales.
- The independent user group embraced the program and encouraged their members to join.
- The open-ended comments from the members were highly positive about the usefulness and relationship value of the program.
- ICON became a catalyst for action and team building within the client.
- ICON assisted in the articulation of the product strategy and near-term plans.
- ICON assisted in drawing together a number of diverse marketing and sales programs, thereby assisting in reducing customer and channel partner fatigue.

INDEX

ABOUT THE AUTHOR

Harry Bunn lives in Princeton New Jersey with his wife and two sons. He is the President & CEO of RONIN Corporation, a marketing consulting and research firm focusing on Business-to-business companies, in particular in the Technology Sector.

He has consulted to many of the largest companies including IBM, Hewlett-Packard, Microsoft, Dell, VMware, EMC, Samsung, AT&T, Verizon, BT, Telefonica, Honeywell, Motorola, Accenture, Nokia, Siemens, Fujitsu and Xerox.

He has written a number of articles for Chief Executive Magazine and other publications and has spoken at a wide range of conferences.

About RONIN Development Corporation

RONIN is a marketing consulting and research company that addresses the needs of large corporations as well as research agencies through a portfolio of services designed for Information Technology, Healthcare and Business-to-Business requirements.

The firm was established in 1986 and works globally, employing a centralized operations model for consistent implementation and a one-stop-shop service. Typically undertaking the most challenging assignments from our clients, we deliver insightful, thorough and accurate results.

9644267R00109

Printed in Great Britain
by Amazon.co.uk, Ltd.,
Marston Gate.